STUDENT **4** BOOK

Get Together

Susan Iannuzzi • David McKeegan

with Ieda Yamasaki-Souza

OXFORD
UNIVERSITY PRESS

Contents

	GRAMMAR	VOCABULARY	FUNCTIONS	FOCUS
Unit 9 **Clarissa has helped me a lot today.** Page 41	Present perfect: statements Present perfect vs. simple past	School subjects	Talking about past experiences	**Reading:** An article for a school newspaper **Writing:** A description of a new student
Unit 10 **Have you ever been in a play?** Page 45	Present perfect: *yes/no* questions and short answers; *ever/never*	Directions words (north, south, east, west)	Describing locations on a map	**Listening:** A conversation **Writing/Speaking:** A description of places you have visited
Rewind Units 9 & 10				
Unit 11 **She hasn't seen her since 1981!** Page 51	Present perfect: *since* and *for*; information questions	Shapes	Asking questions about the past	**Reading:** A conversation **Writing:** A description of a problem
Unit 12 **I haven't met her yet.** Page 55	Present perfect: *already*, *yet*, and *just*	Phrasal verbs	Talking about the past	**Writing:** A description of past activities
Rewind Units 11 & 12				
Unit 13 **You're Rose's friend, aren't you?** Page 61	Affirmative and negative tag questions with *be*: simple present and simple past	Sense verbs	Asking and answering tag questions Giving opinions	**Listening:** Dialog **Writing:** Describe how you felt when a friend left
Unit 14 **You still like me, don't you?** Page 65	Tag questions: simple present and simple past	Swimming accessories	Asking and answering tag questions	**Writing/Speaking:** Write about friends and check information with tag questions
Rewind Units 13 & 14				
Unit 15 **It's a document that shows your country.** Page 71	Relative clauses: *who* and *that*	Personal care items (shampoo, brush, etc.)	Describing people and objects	**Listening:** Descriptions of people **Writing:** A description of your family
Unit 16 **There's a surprise party for Rose!** Page 75	Relative clauses: *where* Review of tenses	Places in a town	Describing places	**Reading:** An e-mail
Rewind Units 15 & 16				

Unit 1 — A cat followed us home!

1 🎧 **Read quickly. What does *alone* mean? Circle the correct answer. Then listen.**

a with many people   **b** with some people   **c** with no people

RAY: The movie was great! Did you like it, Matt?

MATT: Sure! The stunts were great! How about you, Gina?

GINA: I was bored. But Bart Marrs was good...

MATT: Hey, look! That cat is following us. I saw him two hours ago!

RAY: Where did you see him?

MATT: In front of the movie theater. He was alone! Maybe he's lost! Or he doesn't have an owner! Can I pick him up?

GINA: OK, Matt. But be careful. Come on. Let's show him to Mom and Dad.

MATT: Yay! I'll call him Benny.

Got it?

> **Tip**
>
> ***Can* for permission and possibility**
>
> **Can** I pick him up? = permission
>
> **Can** you pick up that box for me? = possibility

2 **Read the conversation again. Answer the questions.**

1 Did Matt enjoy the movie?   — <u>Yes, he did.</u>

2 Did Gina have fun at the movie?   — _____

3 Did Ray see the cat two hours ago?   — _____

4 Is the cat following the kids?   — _____

Focus on language!

Review: simple past

AFFIRMATIVE STATEMENTS	NEGATIVE STATEMENTS
We **saw** a movie yesterday.	We **didn't see** a movie yesterday.
YES/NO QUESTIONS	INFORMATION QUESTIONS
Did you **like** that book? — Yes, I **did**. — No, I **didn't**.	Where/When/Why **did** you **go** yesterday? What/Who **did** you **see** yesterday?

REMEMBER: Irregular verbs: go ⟶ went; see ⟶ saw; give ⟶ gave; make ⟶ made; take ⟶ took; eat ⟶ ate; buy ⟶ bought; have ⟶ had

3 Write the simple past of the verbs below in affirmative and negative form.

	AFFIRMATIVE	NEGATIVE		AFFIRMATIVE	NEGATIVE
buy	bought	didn't buy	give	_____	_____
cook	_____	_____	go	_____	_____
have	_____	_____	make	_____	_____

4 Change the sentences to the simple past. Use the words in parentheses.

1 Dad usually has coffee in the morning. *(juice, this morning)*

Dad had juice this morning.

2 Mom usually makes eggs for breakfast. *(fruit salad, last Saturday morning)*

_____

3 We usually visit Grandma on Saturdays. *(Grandpa, last Saturday)*

_____

4 They usually buy pizza for dinner every Friday. *(hamburgers, last Friday)*

_____

5 My parents usually give me books on my birthday. *(a video game, on my last birthday)*

_____

6 Bill usually takes his motorcycle to work. *(his bicycle, yesterday morning)*

_____

(5) **Fill in the blanks with questions in the simple past.**

MOM: Hi, kids. <u>What movie did you see?</u> <u>Did you like it?</u>
(**1** *What movie / you / see?*) (**2** *you / like / it*)

RAY: We saw *The Stuntman's Reward*. It was great!

MOM: _____
(**3** *Who / you / see / in the movie?*)

GINA: Bart Marrs. Um...we found something while we were

walking home.

DAD: _____
(**4** *What / you / find?*)

MATT: We found a cat, Dad! A beautiful cat!

MOM: Oh, my! _____
(**5** *Where / you / find him?*)

RAY: In front of the movie theater. He followed us home.

DAD: _____
(**6** *you / look for his owner?*)

MATT: Yes, we did. The cat was alone. Can we keep him?

MOM: Well, maybe the cat has an owner, Matt. We can't keep him.

(6) **Look at the pictures below. Write questions and answers. Use the words in parentheses.**

1 <u>Where did Matt go?</u> — <u>He went to the supermarket.</u>
   (*Where / Matt / go?*)   (*the supermarket*)

2 _____ — _____
   (*When / he / go?*)   (*five minutes ago*)

3 _____ — _____
   (*What / he / buy?*)   (*cat food*)

4 _____ — _____
   (*Where / Ray / go?*)   (*the movie theater*)

5 _____ — _____
   (*When / he / go?*)   (*twenty minutes ago*)

6 _____ — _____
   (*Who / he / look for?*)   (*cat's owner*)

7 Read the paragraph and look at the picture. Fill in the blanks with the words in the box.

| tail | back | patch | paws | fur |

The cat's ___back___ is black. He has soft
(1)

___fur___. He has a white _____
(2)   (3)

on his leg. He has four white _____.
                                    (4)

His _____ is long and black.
      (5)

8 Read the paragraph. Then complete the notice with words or phrases from the paragraph. Do not use complete sentences.

Ray, Matt, and Gina found a cat last night on Isabella Avenue, in front of the Trimax Theater. The cat is black, with a white patch on his leg. He has four white paws. Call 555-6351 for information.

FOUND: a cat
DESCRIPTION:
_____
_____
WHERE FOUND:
_____
CALL FOR INFORMATION:
_____

9 Look at exercises 7 and 8. Circle the correct word in parentheses.

1 The cat has (two / *four*) white paws.

2 The kids found the cat on (Trimax / Isabella) Avenue.

3 The cat has a (black / white) patch on his leg.

4 555-6351 is (the kids' / Trimax Theater's) telephone number.

Put it together!

10 In your notebook, write a paragraph about something you found. Describe the thing. What did you do when you found it?

Example I found a wallet on the street last year. It was expensive, and it was beautiful. The owner's name and telephone number were in the wallet. I called the number...

Unit 2

We're not going to keep the cat.

① **Read quickly. How many names does the cat have? Find the cat's real name. Then listen.**

RAY: What were you doing at 2 o'clock this morning, Matt?

MATT: I was sleeping.

GINA: No, you weren't. You were playing with the cat. I found this ball outside your bedroom this morning!

MATT: OK, OK! I was playing with Benny. He was funny! I was laughing!

GINA: We're not going to keep him, Matt. We can't. I'm disappointed, too.... We're all going to miss him.

MATT: I know...hey, wait! Look at this!

RAY: Black fur...a white patch! That's Benny.

MATT: His real name is Giggles! I can't believe it! I'm not going to call him that! His name is Benny.

Lost Cat

Black fur, white patch on leg, white paws, black tail.

Answers to:"Giggles"
Please call: Clara at **555-6456**.

Got it?

② **Read the dialog again. Match the beginnings (1–4) and ends (A–D) of the sentences.**

1 At 2 A.M., Matt wasn't ⎯⎯⎯⎯⎯⎯⎯⎯⎯⎯
2 This morning Gina found
3 Gina and Matt are
4 The owner's number is

    A 555-6456.
    B sleeping.
    C a ball.
    D disappointed.

Focus on language!

Review: past progressive statements

SUBJECT	+	BE	+	VERB + -ING
I		was (not)		
You		were (not)		sleeping when Giggles came in.
He/She/It		was (not)		
We				
You		were (not)		sleeping when Giggles came in.
They				

singular — I / You / He/She/It

plural — We / You / They

3 Look at the picture. What were the people doing at 8 o'clock this morning? Write sentences using the verbs below.

play   run   read   drink   eat

1 The cat _____ was running under the table.

2 Matt _____ .

3 Mom and Ray _____ .

4 Dad _____ .

5 Gina _____ .

4 Look at the picture again. What were the people NOT doing at 8 A.M.? In your notebook, write negative sentences. Use your imagination!

Example   Gina wasn't sleeping at 8 A.M.

6

Review: future with *be + going to*

SUBJECT	+	BE	+	GOING TO	+	VERB
I		am/'m (not)				
He/She/It		is/'s (is not/isn't)		going to		**leave** tonight.
We/You/They		are/'re (are not/aren't)				

5 Fill in the blanks with *be + going to* and the verb in parentheses.

1 I 'm not going to call my cousin today.
(not / call)

2 You _____ the game tomorrow.
(win)

3 We _____ some new CDs this afternoon.
(buy)

4 He _____ home at 4 o'clock.
(come)

5 I _____ baseball tomorrow afternoon.
(not / play)

6 Look at the pictures and captions. Then fill in the blanks with the correct words.

embarrassed	thrilled	worried	disappointed	relieved

"Oops!"	"Great!"	"Oh, is he OK?"	"We'll miss him…"	"What a relief!"

GINA: Hi! Is this Clara? My brothers and I found Benny. Oops! Not Benny! We found

Giggles. Sorry. I'm so ___embarrassed___.
(1)

CLARA: Oh, is he OK? I'm very _____ about him.
(2)

GINA: He's fine. He's at our house.

CLARA: What a relief! I thought he was hurt, but he isn't! I'm so _____.
(3)

GINA: We can take him to your house today.

CLARA: Great! I live on 145 Beech Street. I'm going to see Giggles again! I'm so

_____!
(4)

GINA: We love the cat, too, so we're a little sad and _____.
(5)

We'll miss Giggles, but maybe we can visit him.

7   **Read Matt's e-mail to a friend.**

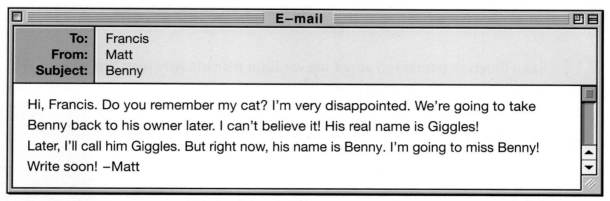

E–mail

To: Francis
From: Matt
Subject: Benny

Hi, Francis. Do you remember my cat? I'm very disappointed. We're going to take Benny back to his owner later. I can't believe it! His real name is Giggles! Later, I'll call him Giggles. But right now, his name is Benny. I'm going to miss Benny! Write soon! –Matt

Now read the sentences. Circle _T_ (_True_) or _F_ (_False_).

1 The kids are not going to take the cat to his owner later.	**T /Ⓕ**
2 Matt isn't going to miss the cat.	**T / F**
3 Matt is disappointed because the cat is going to stay with him.	**T / F**
4 Matt likes the cat's real name.	**T / F**
5 Matt will call the cat Giggles later.	**T / F**

8   **Correct the false sentences in exercise 7.**

1 <u>The kids are going to take the cat to his owner later.</u> _____

2 _____

3 _____

4 _____

9   **Work in pairs. Think of five surprising things. Tell them to your partner. Practice _I can't believe it!_**

Example   **STUDENT A:** I'm going to visit Mount Everest next summer.

               STUDENT B: I can't believe it!

> **Tip**
>
> _I can't believe it!_
> **A:** His name is Giggles!
> **B:** I can't believe it!
> We use the phrase _**I can't believe it**_ to express surprise.

Put it together!

10   **When were you embarrassed? Write about what happened in your notebook.**

Example   I was in a store with my friends when I saw my favorite actor. He smiled at me, and I smiled at him and waved. But then I walked into a wall! I was so embarrassed!

Rewind

Units 1&2

1 Read Dennis's paragraph about his vacation with his wife Joan last year. Change the verbs in parentheses to the simple past.

We ___had___ a great vacation last year. We _____ to England.
(**1** have)   (**2** go)

The weather was beautiful! It _____. We
(**3** not / rain)

_____ in a big hotel in London, and we _____ a lot of
(**4** stay)   (**5** see)

interesting things. Joan's favorite place was the Tower of

London, but I _____ it.
(**6** not / like)

2 Read the paragraph again. Answer the questions. Use short answers.

1 Did Dennis and Joan enjoy their vacation?   —   Yes, they did.

2 Was the weather terrible?   —   _____

3 Did they stay in a small hotel?   —   _____

4 Was the Tower of London Joan's favorite place? —   _____

3 Write questions about Dennis and Joan. Use *Who*, *What*, *Where*, or *When*.

1 _When did Dennis and Joan go_ to England?   — They went to England last year.

2 _____ stay?   — They stayed in a big hotel.

3 _____ like?   — She liked the Tower of London.

4 _____ the Tower of London?   — Dennis didn't like it.

4 Label the parts of the dog's body.

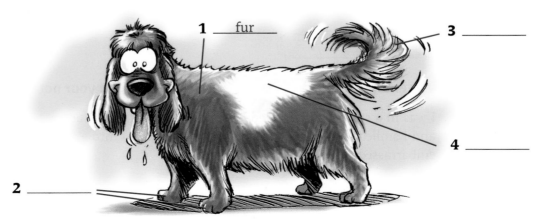

1 ___fur___   3 _____

4 _____

2 _____

9

⑤ Change the verbs in parentheses to the past progressive.

1 The children ___were swimming___ (*swim*) in the lake at 3 P.M. yesterday.

2 I _____ (*watch*) TV when the thunder started.

3 Tom was cold last night because he _____ (*not / wear*) a coat.

4 You _____ (*sleep*) when I called you.

5 Troy _____ (*stand*) outside when we opened the door.

⑥ Look at the pictures. What is or is not going to happen? Use the words in the box.

> **dive into the pool**   **rain**   **play baseball**   **buy the dress**

1 It ___is going to rain___ .

3 They _____ .

2 She _____ .

4 He _____ .

⑦ Imagine you are in the situations below. How do you feel? Use the words in the box.

> **disappointed**   **worried**   **relieved**   **embarrassed**   **thrilled**

1 The mail carrier gives you a big box. You feel ___thrilled___ .

2 You open the box. There's nothing inside it. You feel _____ .

3 You can't find your dog. You feel _____ .

4 You see a tail behind a tree in the yard. It's your dog. You feel _____ .

5 You don't know the words to a song. Your friends laugh. You feel _____ .

Unit 3 — I used to be afraid of this house.

1 🎧 **Read quickly. What does *creepy* mean? Circle the correct answer. Then listen.**

a beautiful   **b** difficult   **c** scary

MATT: Maybe the owner will give us a reward.

GINA: That's not important, Matt.... Hey, stop here, guys. This is the address.

MATT: Oh, no! Not that house! I don't like it.

RAY: I don't, either.

GINA: Why? What's wrong with it?

RAY: Well, I used to be afraid of this house when I was a little kid. My friends and I used to run when we passed it. It's a little creepy.

GINA: You're silly. I think this house is pretty. Come on, let's go in.

MATT: I'm scared. Can I stay here?

GINA: No, Matt! Don't be ridiculous. We'll go in together.

Got it?

2 **Read the conversation again. Write short answers.**

1 Who's afraid of the house?   — <u>Matt.</u>

2 Who used to be afraid of the house?   — _____

3 Is Gina afraid?   — _____

4 Who lives in the house?   — _____

3 **Find words in the conversation with the same meaning as the words below.**

1 scary   = <u>   creepy   </u>   **3** beautiful   = _____

2 scared   = _____   **4** silly   = _____

11

Focus on language!

Used to and didn't use to

	SUBJECT	+	USE(D) TO	+	VERB
affirmative	I		used to		be very heavy. I'm thinner now.
	He		used to		live in Germany. Now he lives in England.
	We		used to		wake up early. We wake up late now.
negative	You		didn't use to		study every day. You study every day now.
	She		didn't use to		like pizza. She likes it now.
	They		didn't use to		like pop music. They love it now.

4 Fill in the blanks with *used to* or *didn't use to* and the words in parentheses.

1 Joe _____ used to be _____ short when he was 12. He's very tall now.
         (be)

2 I _____ _____ fish. Now it's my favorite food.
         (not / like)

3 He _____ _____ the subway to work. Now he drives to work.
         (take)

4 We _____ _____ jeans. Now we wear them every day.
         (not / wear)

5 She _____ _____ classical music. She loves it now.
         (not / enjoy)

6 They _____ _____ the floor three times a week. Now they don't.
         (mop)

5 Look at the chart. Fill in the blanks with *used to* or *didn't use to*.

	FIVE YEARS AGO	NOW
Ray	play drums	play the violin
Gina	watch cartoons	watch comedy shows
Matt	eat bananas	eat steak

1 Ray _____ used to _____ play the drums. He doesn't play them now.

2 Ray _____ didn't use to _____ play the violin. He plays it now.

3 Gina _____ watch cartoons. She doesn't watch them now.

4 Gina _____ watch comedy shows. She watches them now.

5 Matt _____ eat steak. He eats it now.

6 Matt _____ eat bananas. He doesn't eat them now.

6 **Look at the picture. Read the conversation.**

> **RAY:** Is she at home, Gina? Are you sure?
> **GINA:** Yes, she is. Ring the doorbell again, Ray.
> **RAY:** I don't think it's working. Knock on the door, Matt.
> **MATT:** I'm scared, but OK.... I'll knock. No answer. I don't think she's here.
> **RAY:** I don't, either! Let's go!
> **GINA:** Wait...I think she's coming now! She's looking through the peephole.
> **CLARA:** Yes? Who's there?... Oh, hello, kids!

Now match the phrases with the numbers in the picture.

ring the doorbell _3_   knock on the door __   look through the peephole __

7 **What do you think? Read the statements and look at the responses in parentheses. Circle the answers that are correct for you.**

1 I don't like shrimp.   — (*I don't, either! / I do!*)
2 I love comedy shows.   — (*I do, too! / I don't!*)
3 I like soccer.   — (*I do, too! / I don't!*)
4 I don't like video games.   — (*I don't, either! / I do!*)
5 I don't like creepy houses. — (*I don't, either! / I do!*)

Tip

	Agree	Disagree
I **like** cheese.	— I do, too!	I don't!
I **don't like** soda.	— I don't, either!	I do!

Use *...too!* to agree with positive statements.
Use *not...either!* to agree with negative statements.

Review: future with *will*

SUBJECT	+	*WILL*	+	*(NOT)*	+	VERB
I / You						
He / She / It		will/'ll		(not)		miss Giggles.
We / You / They						

NOTE: *will not = won't*

---

8 **What will happen? Fill in the blanks with *will* or *won't* and the verbs in parentheses.**

Giggles ___won't live___ with the kids in the future. His owner and Giggles ___will be___
  (1 *not / live***)**   **(2** *be***)**

happy together. Matt _____ Giggles, but the kids _____ him
                                   (3 *miss***)**   **(4** *visit***)**

sometimes. Clara _____ lunch for the kids, and Matt _____
                          (5 *make***)**   **(6** *play***)**

with Giggles. And Giggles _____ his home again!
                                      (7 *not / leave***)**

9 🎧 **Listen to the dialog. Circle the correct picture.**

1

2

3

10 **Write sentences with *used to* and the words in parentheses. Then match them with the pictures above.**

1 <u>The woman used to be a movie star and an athlete.</u>
(The woman / be / a movie star and an athlete)

Picture <u>3</u>

2 _____ . Now she can't run very fast.
(The woman / be / an athlete)

Picture __

3 _____ . Now she's a painter.
(The woman / be / a dancer)

Picture __

Put it together!

11 **In groups, talk about what you used to do when you were younger. Fill in the chart with information about three of your classmates.**

NAME	USED TO ...	DIDN'T USE TO ...
<u>Paula</u>	<u>cry a lot</u>	<u>like sports</u>
STUDENT A: _____	_____	_____
STUDENT B: _____	_____	_____
STUDENT C: _____	_____	_____

Unit 4   Did you enjoy yourselves?

(1) 🎧 **Read quickly. What is Clara's surprise for the kids? Guess! Then listen.**

MOM: Hi, kids! Did you enjoy yourselves at the pool?

GINA: It was great, but Matt didn't behave himself!

RAY: He was running too fast, and he fell and hurt himself.

MOM: Oh, no! Did you cut yourself? Let me help you.

MATT: Mom, it's a small cut! I'm fine! I can take care of myself.

MOM: OK, Matt. Kids, you're all wet! Dry yourselves in the bathroom. It's time for lunch....
Oh, please answer the phone, dear.

DAD: Kids, it's your friend Clara. She's going to visit us this afternoon.

MATT: Cool! Is Giggles going to come with her?

DAD: Well, no...but she has a surprise for you...

Got it?

(2) **Read the conversation again. Put the sentences in order to make a summary. Then write the sentences in the correct order in your notebook.**

___ The kids ate lunch.

___ Ray, Gina, and Matt came home from the pool.

___ Clara called.

_1_ Matt hurt himself.

___ Dad answered the phone.

15

Focus on language!

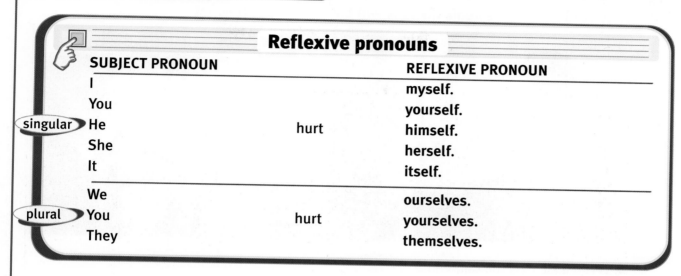

Reflexive pronouns

SUBJECT PRONOUN		REFLEXIVE PRONOUN
I		myself.
You		yourself.
singular He	hurt	himself.
She		herself.
It		itself.
We		ourselves.
plural You	hurt	yourselves.
They		themselves.

③ **Match the subjects with the correct reflexive pronouns.**

A yourselves	C itself	E himself	G herself
B myself	D themselves	F ourselves	H yourself

C **1** the animal

— **2** I

— **3** Gina and Matt

— **4** you and your friends

— **5** my brother and I

— **6** Mom

— **7** Dad

— **8** you (*singular*)

④ **Write sentences using the words in parentheses and the correct reflexive pronouns.**

1 <u>My sister can't take care of herself.</u>
  (*My sister / can / not / take care of*)

2 _____
  (*The baby boy / can / not / wash*)

3 _____
  (*We / did / not / hurt*)

4 _____
  (*The kids / dried*)

5 _____
  (*I / burned*)

6 _____
  (*You / cut*)

7 _____
  (*You and Ali / did / not / behave*)

8 _____
  (*The animal / did / not / hurt*)

5 Read the conversation and look at the picture. Then look at 1-6 below and put a check (✓) next to the items the kids will buy at the supermarket.

MATT: Please pass the salt, Gina.

GINA: Here you are. Can you pass me the pepper, Ray?

RAY: OK. Mom, I need some mustard, but there's only a little in this jar. Do we have any more?

DAD: And I need a little salad dressing for my salad, but I can't find any.

MOM: Sorry, we don't have any more mustard or salad dressing. I need some soy sauce, too, and a few other things. Kids would you like to go to the supermarket for me before Clara arrives?

DAD: And remember...buy a lot of cat food.

MATT: Cat food? Why?

1 mustard ✓   **3** pepper —   **5** soy sauce —

2 salt —   **4** cat food —   **6** salad dressing —

6 Read Mom's shopping list. Look at the Tip. Then, in your notebook, answer the questions.

shopping
1 small bottle of salad dressing
15 cans of cat food
1 small bottle of ketchup
1 small jar of mustard
1 big bottle of soy sauce
4 eggs

Example   Does Mom need a lot of eggs?

No, she doesn't. She needs a few eggs.

1 Does she need a few cans of cat food?
2 Does she need a lot of ketchup?
3 Does she need a lot of mustard?
4 Does she need a lot of salad dressing?
5 Does she need a little soy sauce?

Tip

a few
Use with countable nouns.

a few potatoes

a little
Use with uncountable nouns.

a little ketchup

a lot of
Use with countable and uncountable nouns.

a lot of potatoes
a lot of ketchup

(7) **Look at pictures A-C and sentences 1-6. Which picture does each sentence describe? Write the letter of the picture on the line next to each number.**

A  B 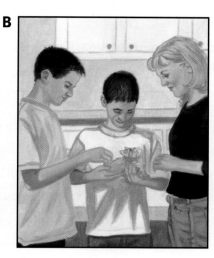 C

  A **1** Clara was in the kitchen. She had a present for the kids!

  — **2** The kids enjoyed themselves with their new kitten. Matt was thrilled!

  — **3** Ray was unlocking the door when Dad called their names. He told them to come into the kitchen.

  — **4** Clara's present for the kids was a little kitten!

  — **5** Matt held the cute kitten in his arms.

  — **6** Ray, Gina, and Matt came back from the supermarket.

(8) **Look at the pictures again. Which happened first, second, and third? Write the letters of the pictures on the lines below.**

First: C   **Second:** _____   **Third:** _____

(9) **Look at exercises 7 and 8 again. Now write the story in your notebook. Use your own words.**

Example   The kids came home. They opened the door...

Put it together!

(10) **In your notebook, write about a time when you enjoyed yourself a lot. Share this experience with the class.**

Example   I went with my friends to a rock concert. The band was great...

Rewind

Units 3 & 4

(1) Gordon didn't have a lot of money ten years ago. But he worked a lot, and now he has more money. Today his life is very different.

TEN YEARS AGO	TODAY
He didn't have a car.	He drives a big car.
He lived in a small house.	He lives in a big house.
He worked every day.	He doesn't work every day.
He didn't eat in restaurants.	He eats in expensive restaurants.
He got up at 6 A.M. every day.	He doesn't get up early in the morning.

Complete the sentences with *used to* or *didn't use to* and the correct verb.

1 <u>He didn't use to have a car</u>   , but today he has a big car.

2 _____ , but today he lives in a big house.

3 _____ , but today he doesn't work every day.

4 _____ , but today he eats in expensive restaurants.

5 _____ , but today he doesn't get up early in the morning.

(2) **Jackie and Diana are classmates. Complete the conversation with *I do, too* or *I don't, either*.**

JACKIE: I like school.

DIANA: (1) <u>I do, too.</u>   But I don't like math very much.

JACKIE: (2) <u>I don't, either.</u>   And I don't like geography very much.

DIANA: (3) _____

Art is my favorite subject. I love it!

JACKIE: (4) _____

I like our teacher.

DIANA: (5) _____

But I don't want any homework tonight.

JACKIE: (6) _____

But we are going to get some homework!

3 **Look at the pictures and fill in the blanks with *myself*, *yourself*, *herself*, or *yourselves*.**

1

I cut ___myself___.

3

Did you hurt _____?

2

You two! Behave _____.

4

She loves _____.

4 **Fill in the blanks with *a lot of*, *a few*, or *a little*.**

1 This soup is wonderful, but it needs ___a little___ salt.

2 Jim is very popular. He has _____ friends.

3 I have five jars of mustard. Would you like _____ jars?

4 This library is very big. There are _____ books in it.

5 This park is clean! There is only _____ litter in it!

5 **Listen to the song. Then complete the sentences with *used to* or *didn't use to*.**

I ___used to___ know some movie stars,
    (1)
But now I don't know one.

I _____ have an expensive car,
    (2)
And take vacations in the sun.

But I _____ feel so fine
    (3)
Or see the sky so blue.

I'm happier because you're mine.

Life's better now with you.

20

Unit 5

If they choose me, I'll go to Japan!

1 **Read quickly. Complete the sentence below. Then listen.**

A student representative goes to presentations about ______________.

MOM: Hi, Alex! Tell us about the interview this morning.

ALEX: It was fun! If the committee members choose me, I'll be a student representative. I'll go to the International Teen Conference in Japan and represent the United States!

MOM: You'll be a wonderful student representative. You'll go to presentations and discussions about other countries in the world.

TODD: Yes, the teens at the conference will love your presentation on New Mexico!

ALEX: Thanks.

ERIKA: If they choose you, I'll be very happy, Alex! When will you leave if you become the representative?... Can I borrow your CDs?

Got it?

2 **Read the conversation again. Put a check (√) under *T (True)*, *F (False)*, or *NI (No information)*.**

	T	F	NI
1 Alex is a student representative now.		✓	
2 Alex had an interview today.			
3 Alex is going to be a student representative.			
4 Erika won't be happy if they choose Alex.			

Focus on language!

First conditional: statements

IF + SUBJECT + SIMPLE PRESENT			SUBJECT + *WILL* + VERB		
If	I	**study** hard,	I	**will/'ll**	**be** a good student.
If	he	**doesn't pass** the exam,	he	**won't**	**be** happy.
If	they	**go** to Japan,	they	**won't**	**come** to my party.

3 Fill in the blanks with the correct forms of the verbs in parentheses.

1 If Alex ___leaves___ , Erika ___will borrow___ his CDs.
      (leave)   *(borrow)*

2 If the committee members _____ Alex, he _____ thrilled.
              (choose)   *(be)*

3 If Alex _____ to Japan, his family _____ him.
        (go)   *(miss)*

4 If Alex _____ his CDs with him to Japan, Erika _____ happy.
        (take)   *(not / be)*

5 If his mother _____ the program, Alex _____ to Japan.
        (not / like)   *(not / go)*

4 Write Alex's sentences. Use the words in parentheses.

1 <u>If I become the student representative, I'll meet a lot of people.</u>
    (I - become a student representative / I - meet a lot of people)

2 _____
    (I - travel to Japan / I - fly in an airplane)

3 _____
    (the committee members - not choose me / I - be disappointed)

4 _____
    (I - go on the trip / my friends - not come with me)

5 _____
    (I - stay in Tokyo for a few weeks / I - learn about Japan)

5 Look at the Tip. Then write the sentences from exercise 4 in your notebook with the *if*-clause at the end of the sentence.

Example I'll meet a lot of people if I become a student representative.

Tip

If we win the competition, we'll be thrilled.

We'll be thrilled **if we win the competition**.

The *if*-clause can be the first or last clause in the sentence. When the *if*-clause begins the sentence, a comma comes after it.

6 **Complete the sentences about yourself.**

Example <u>I won't walk to school</u> if it rains tomorrow.

1 _____ if it's sunny tomorrow.

2 _____ if I don't study English tonight.

3 _____ if I go to bed at 12 o'clock.

4 _____ if I go to the party on Saturday.

7 **Fill in the blanks with the correct words. Use the simple present for the verbs.**

mail

receive

deliver

return address

stamp

national Teen Conference

Alex Pedrillo
4500 Mercedes Street
Santa Fe, NM 58888

envelope

ALEX: The committee members always ___mail___ the letters one day after the interview.
(1)

Mom! The mail carrier usually _____ the mail at 1 o'clock. Did I
(2)

_____ any letters today?
(3)

MOM: Yes! There's a letter from the committee!

ALEX: Did you open it? What did it say?

MOM: I didn't open it. I saw the _____ on the _____.
(4)   (5)

ERIKA: Open it carefully, Alex! I want that _____ on the envelope for my collection!
(6)

ALEX: Don't worry! I will!

First conditional: information questions

QUESTION WORD	+	*WILL* CLAUSE	+	*IF*-CLAUSE
What		will you do		if the committee doesn't choose you?
Who		will I meet		if I go to Japan?

8 **Fill in the blanks with questions. Use the words in parentheses.**

ALEX: I'm a little scared. <u>What will I do if they don't choose me?</u>
(**1** What / I do / they / not choose me?)

TODD: Don't worry. They'll choose you. _____
(**2** Who / they choose / they / not choose you?)

ALEX: OK, I'll open it...Yes! I'm going to Japan! My partner at the conference is going to

be the Canadian representative.

TODD: Cool! But... _____
(**3** what / you do / you / not recognize her?)

ALEX: Oh, she'll send me her photo, and I'll send her mine.

We'll do many things together, but we won't stay with

the same Japanese family.

TODD: Really? _____
(**4** Where / you stay / you / not stay with the same family?)

ALEX: I'll stay with the Kawaba family, and she'll stay with the Ikedas.

9 **Read the paragraph about Alex. Complete Alex's information form (1).**

My name is Alex Pedrillo. I'm a student from Santa Fe, New Mexico, in the United States. I live with my parents, my older brother, and my younger sister. I like music and animals, but I don't like video games. In the future, I'll probably make nature documentaries about the environment. I'll be very happy if I can be a student representative at the International Teen Conference in Japan!

1
Name: __Alex Pedrillo__

City and Country: _____

Family: _____

Occupation: _____

Likes: _____

Dislikes: _____

Plans for the Future: _____

_____

2
Name: _____

City and Country: _____

Family: _____

Occupation: _____

Likes: _____

Dislikes: _____

Plans for the Future: _____

_____

Put it together!

10 **Fill in the second form (2) with your information. Then write a paragraph about yourself in your notebook. Use the paragraph about Alex as a model.**

24

Unit 6 — You should read the guidelines.

INTERNATIONAL TEEN CONFERENCE

Guidelines

Congratulations!

Welcome to the International Teen Conference! Please read the following guidelines.

1 You should arrive in Tokyo during the last week of November, but you must arrive before December 1st. The conference will start on December 1st.

2 The weather in Tokyo is usually cold in December. You should bring a coat or jacket. You should also bring clothes for formal occasions.

3 You should always be polite, and you should follow your Japanese host family's instructions at all times. You must contact the Committee with problems.

4 You shouldn't bring any food from your country. Your host family will serve you different kinds of Japanese food, such as *sashimi* (raw fish). Japanese food is delicious!

1 🎧 Read the guidelines above quickly. Circle the adjective that describes Tokyo's weather in December. Then listen.

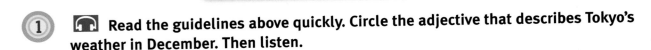

warm   cold   rainy   dry   snowy

ALEX: Look at these guidelines for student representatives!
TODD: Wow! There are a lot of rules. But it'll be fun!

Got it?

2 Read the guidelines again. Complete the sentences.

1 The conference will start on <u>December 1st</u>.

2 Students will need a coat for _____ weather.

3 Students should be _____ to their host families.

4 *Sashimi* is raw _____.

Focus on language!

Should / Shouldn't for advice or recommendation

My clothes are dirty. I **should** wash them.
You'll be late for the movie. You **should** leave now.
He's sick. He **shouldn't** go to school tomorrow.
It's cold. We **shouldn't** wear shorts.

NOTE: *shouldn't = should not*

3 Fill in the blanks with *should* or *shouldn't*.

1 Erika is sick. She _____ should _____ stay home today.

2 This is a dangerous city. We _____ be careful with our bags.

3 His teeth aren't very good. He _____ eat candy.

4 We always get up too late in the morning. We _____ go to bed earlier.

5 They're not hungry. They _____ eat those big bowls of ice cream.

6 My parents are sleeping. I _____ play loud music.

4 Give advice. Use the words from the boxes. Make one sentence with *should* and one with *shouldn't* for each item.

Should
read books in French
go to the doctor
jog or play a sport
study tonight

Shouldn't
go to the rock concert tonight
sleep in French class
eat a lot of chocolate
play tennis this afternoon

1 A: I'm sick today.

B: You should go to the doctor. You shouldn't play tennis this afternoon.

2 A: I have an exam tomorrow.

B: _____

3 A: That old man is very heavy.

B: _____

4 A: She can't speak French very well.

B: _____

5 Give advice to a new student in your class. Write four sentences in your notebook.

Example   You shouldn't bring computer games to class.

6 Match the beginnings (1–4) and ends (A–D) of the sentences.

1 Alex should bring slippers because...
2 Alex should bring a jacket because...
3 Alex should bring a suit and tie because...
4 Alex should bring a belt because...

A he needs clothes for formal occasions.
B it's cold in Tokyo in December.
C he can't wear shoes inside the houses.
D his pants are very big.

Must / Mustn't for rules

SUBJECT	+	MUST (NOT)	+	VERB
I				
You		**must**		**feed** the dog.
He/She/It		**must not/mustn't**		
We/You/They				

---

7 Fill in the blanks in the airport check-in sign with *must* or *must not*.

INSTRUCTIONS FOR TRAVELERS

1 You _____must_____ show your passport.

2 You _____ show your ticket.

3 You _____ take only two bags on the plane.

4 You _____ take large animals on the plane.

5 You _____ carry packages for strangers. It is dangerous.

6 You _____ be late for your flight.

8 Look at exercise 7. Fill in the blanks with *should*, *shouldn't*, *must*, or *mustn't*.

1 Alex _____must_____ bring his passport to the airport.

2 Alex _____ bring shorts and sandals with him. The weather is cold in Tokyo in the winter.

3 Travelers _____ show their tickets.

4 It's going to snow today. You _____ wear your scarf.

5 Alex _____ be late for his flight. The plane won't wait for him if he's late.

9 Read the last page of the guidelines. In your notebook, write the sentences again. Use *should* or *shouldn't*.

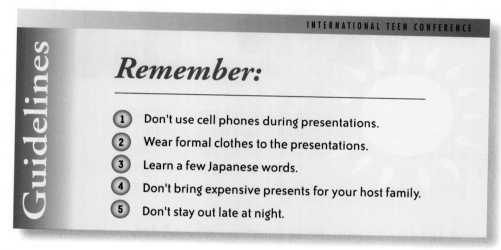

INTERNATIONAL TEEN CONFERENCE

Guidelines

Remember:

1. Don't use cell phones during presentations.
2. Wear formal clothes to the presentations.
3. Learn a few Japanese words.
4. Don't bring expensive presents for your host family.
5. Don't stay out late at night.

Example   People shouldn't use cell phones during presentations.

10 In pairs, discuss the guidelines. Do you agree with them?

Example   A: I agree with number 1. People shouldn't take cell phones to presentations because they're loud.

B: I don't agree with number 1. People need cell phones when there's an emergency.

Put it together!

11 Work in groups. What do you think? What characteristics should a student representative at the International Teen Conference have? Write sentences about a good student representative. Use *should*, *shouldn't*, *must*, or *mustn't*.

Example   A good student representative should know many things about his/her country.

Rewind — Units 5&6

1 What will Brian do tomorrow? Look at the pictures. Then match 1–5 with A–E.

1 If there's a party,   **A** I'll fly my kite in the park.
2 If Lynne calls,   **B** I'll wear my new jeans.
3 If it rains,   **C** I'll meet John at the beach.
4 If it's windy,   **D** I'll take her to a restaurant at 8 P.M.
5 If it's sunny,   **E** I'll stay at home and study.

2 Look at exercise 1 again. Write questions about Brian.

1 What _____will he do if it rains_____ ? — He'll stay at home and study.

2 Who _____ ? — He'll meet John.

3 Where _____ ? — He'll go to the park.

4 When _____ ? — He'll take her to a restaurant at 8 P.M.

5 What _____ ? — He'll wear his new jeans.

3 Circle the correct form of the verbs in parentheses.

1 If you (*mail* / *will mail*) the letter today, they will receive it tomorrow.

2 If they receive the letter tomorrow, they (*is* / *will be*) happy.

3 I (*am* / *will be*) sad if you don't send me a postcard.

4 Your friend (*receives* / *won't receive*) the card if the address is wrong.

5 If it (*is* / *will be*) a nice stamp, I'll put it in my collection.

4 Tracy wants to be a professional basketball player. What *should* she do? What *shouldn't* she do? Complete the sentences below.

1 _____She should_____ play basketball every day.

2 _____ stay in bed all day on the weekends.

3 _____ eat good food.

4 _____ drink a lot of milk shakes.

5 _____ go to parties every night.

6 _____ do a lot of exercise.

5 Look at the rules of the Teen Camp. Write sentences about what the teens *must* and *mustn't* do. Use the words in parentheses.

1 _They must get up at 8 A.M._
(*get up*)

2 _____
(*run*)

3 _____
(*play*)

4 _____
(*wash*)

5 _____
(*go to bed*)

TEEN RULES

DO...
- get up at 8 A.M.
- wash your dishes.
- keep the dining room clean.
- go to bed early.

DON'T...
- run in the dining room.
- walk in the forest alone.
- play music after 9 P.M.

6 Label the pictures. Then fill in the numbers in the alphabet code.

1

S L I P P E R S
8 15 18 11 11 22 9 8

3

_ _ _ _
25 22 15 7

5

_ _ _
7 18 22

2

_ _ _ _ _ _ _
8 4 22 26 7 22 9

4

_ _ _ _
8 6 18 7

A	B	C	D	E	F	G	H	I	J	K	L	M
_	_	_	_	22	_	_	_	18	_	_	15	_

N	O	P	Q	R	S	T	U	V	W	X	Y	Z
_	_	11	_	9	8	_	_	_	_	_	_	_

Unit 7

We might study Japanese.

To: Todd
From: Alex
Subject: International Teen Conference

Dear Todd,

I'm having a fantastic time! Here's a picture of Laura, the Canadian representative. She's great. We might take some Japanese language classes. We don't have to speak Japanese because a lot of Japanese people know English, but Laura and I will learn a few Japanese words before we leave.

The other picture is of the Kawabas. They are a wonderful host family. Mrs. Kawaba cooks excellent shrimp. Japanese people often use chopsticks, but I don't have to use them because the Kawabas gave me a fork and a knife! I wear my slippers every day because I have to take off my shoes in the house.

We're going to give our presentations tomorrow! It'll be fun!

Alex

---

(1) 🎧 **Read the e-mail above quickly. Circle the correct answer. Then listen.**

The Japanese often use chopsticks. They usually don't use (*forks and knives / salt and pepper*).

Got it?

(2) **Read the e-mail again. Then look at sentences 1-5. Fill in the blanks with the correct names.**

1 _____Laura_____ is from Canada.

2 _____ and _____ will learn a few Japanese words.

3 _____ cooks well.

4 _____ eats with a fork and a knife.

(3) **Work in groups. Look at the facts about Japan in Alex's e-mail. What is the same and what is different in your country? Discuss.**

Focus on language!

Have to / Don't have to for obligation or necessity

		SUBJECT +	*HAVE TO* +	VERB
affirmative	The ketchup bottle is empty.	I	have to	buy a new bottle.
	He's not doing well in school.	He	has to	study more.
negative	It's a holiday today.	We	don't have to	go to school.
	There's the tram.	She	doesn't have to	walk home.

4 **Write sentences. Use the correct form of *have to* and the words in parentheses.**

1 Alex's presentation will be tomorrow. <u>He has to prepare it tonight.</u>
(He / prepare it tonight)

2 Laura's family has slippers for her. _____
(She / not buy any)

3 Everyone at the conference speaks English.

_____
(They / not speak Japanese)

4 Laura's parents are waiting for a phone call from her.

_____
(She / call her parents today)

5 **Fill in the blanks with the correct form of *have to*.**

LAURA: It's Sunday tomorrow. We ____<u>don't have to</u>____ wake
(1)

up early, and we _____ go to the
(2)

conference! Why don't we go to the movies?

ALEX: Well, I _____ go out for lunch with
(3)

the Kawabas. We're having *tempura*.... Hey, would you like to come with us?

LAURA: Cool! Thanks! But I _____ be home at 5 o'clock because I
(4)

_____ call my parents in Canada.
(5)

ALEX: OK...oh, I'll call you later. I _____ go now because Mr. Kawaba
(6)

_____ use the phone.
(7)

6 **Look at the pictures. Fill in the blanks with the correct vegetable name.**

MR. KAWABA: What kind of *tempura* would you like?

LAURA: I'm not sure...how about some with __eggplant__ ?
(1)

MR. KAWABA: Sorry, my English... What's "eggplant"?

ALEX: It's a big purple vegetable.

MRS. KAWABA: And those small white vegetables? Those are _____ , (2) right? We can have *tempura* with them, and with the green vegetable ... Uh, _____ ? (3)

LAURA: Yes, that's right! I like *tempura* with _____ . You know, the orange vegetables. (4)

MR. KAWABA: OK, let's have *tempura* with mushrooms, broccoli, carrots, and...oh, no! What's the big yellow and brown thing? Oh, and with _____ ! I just remembered! (5)

onion

eggplant

carrots

mushrooms

broccoli

Might / Might not for possibility

SUBJECT	+	*MIGHT (NOT)*	+	VERB
I/You/He/She/It We/You/They		might (not)		study Japanese.

---

7 **In your notebook, rewrite the sentences. Use *might* or *might not*.**

Example Maybe it won't rain tomorrow. <u>It might not rain tomorrow.</u>

1 Maybe we'll go to a movie on Friday.
2 Maybe he'll make eggplant *tempura* next week.
3 Maybe they won't want broccoli for lunch today.
4 Maybe you won't have an exam tomorrow.

8 Read the conference program. Then look at Alex's notes (√ = *have to go*; ? = *might go*). Fill in the blanks with the correct form of *have to* or *might*.

1 Alex ____might____ go to the presentation on Egypt.

2 Alex _____ go to the presentation on New Mexico in the United States. He's going to give the presentation!

3 Alex _____ go to the slideshow on Ghana.

4 Alex _____ go to the group dinner at the Korean restaurant.

5 Alex _____ go to Laura's presentation on Canadian teens.

6 Alex _____ go to the Japanese drums performance.

DECEMBER 7	CONFERENCE PROGRAM	
Morning 10 A.M.	Presentation: "Exciting Egypt" —Aya Maksoud	?
11 A.M.	Presentation: "Focus on New Mexico, USA" —Alex Pedrillo	√
Afternoon 1:00 P.M.	Presentation: "Canadian Teens" —Laura Purnell	√
4:00 P.M.	Slideshow: "Life in Accra, Ghana" —Daniel Igbo	?
Evening 7:00 P.M.	Group dinner at Korean restaurant	√
9:00 P.M.	Japanese drums performance	?

9 Look at the conference program again. In your notebook, write a paragraph about Alex. Use *has to* and *doesn't have to*.

Example In the morning, Alex doesn't have to go to the presentation on Egypt...

10 Look at the program again. Imagine you are going to the conference tomorrow. What presentations might **you** go to? Write sentences in your notebook.

Example I might go to the presentation on New Mexico.

Put it together!

11 In your notebook, make a schedule for tomorrow. What do you *have to* do tomorrow, and what *might* you do? Write a paragraph about your activities.

Example I have to get up at 7 A.M. tomorrow. I might eat some bread at 8 A.M. I have to go to school...

Unit 8 — Learning about the world is fun.

EGYPT

1 Enjoying the sun and water

Scuba diving in the Red Sea is exhilarating. You can swim underwater and see coral and exotic fish!

2 Walking around in the cities of Egypt is exciting. The architecture is beautiful. There are plenty of things to buy, and the people are friendly.

3 Visiting the Pyramids is fascinating. The Pyramids are the most popular tourist attractions in Egypt. Thousands of people visit them every year.

---

1 🎧 **Read the poster quickly. Fill in the blanks with headings _a–c_. Then listen.**

a Enjoying the cities **b** Enjoying the sun and water **c** Enjoying the most popular places for tourists

LAURA: This presentation about Egypt is really interesting!... Aya, how far are the Pyramids from Cairo?

AYA: They're not far. The Pyramids are in Giza, and Giza is part of Cairo.

ALEX: And is riding popular in Egypt? Do people ride camels?

AYA: Yes, but not in the cities, of course! People usually travel by car, bus, taxi, and motorcycle in the cities.

ALEX: Gee, I really want to learn more about Egypt!

Got it?

2 **Read the poster again. Match the words with their meanings.**

1 exhilarating
2 exotic
3 popular
4 plenty of

A a lot of
B many people like it
C thrilling and exciting
D different

3 **What do you think people from other countries know or don't know about your country? Think of three things. Tell your classmates.**

Example   People from other countries don't know about my country's beaches.

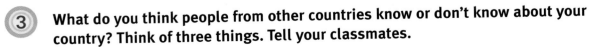

Focus on language!

Gerunds

We **swim** every day.   swim = verb

Swimming is fun.   swimming = gerund (noun) - subject

Aya loves **swimming**.   swimming = gerund (noun) - object

To form the gerund:

For verbs ending in *-e*, drop the *-e* and add *-ing*: *dancing, using*.

For verbs ending in one vowel + one consonant, double the consonant

before the *-ing*: *sitting, digging*.

---

4   **Fill in the blanks with the gerunds of the verbs in parentheses.**

1   <u>Eating</u>   *sashimi* is popular in Japan.
    (eat)

2   I finished _____ that book yesterday.
                 (read)

3   _____ is exhilarating.
      (win)

4   These athletes are famous for _____ fast.
                             (run)

5   _____ at home can be fun!
      (stay)

6   _____ is easy.
      (cook)

5   **Write sentences using the words in parentheses. Include a gerund in each sentence.**

1   <u>Learning about other countries is fun.</u>
           (Learn about other countries / be / fun)

2   _____
           (Listen to presentations / be / great)

3   _____
           (Share with other people / be / good)

4   _____
           (Pack carefully / be / a good idea)

5   _____
           (Every year they discuss / visit the Pyramids in Egypt)

6   _____
           (They finish / make sashimi / an hour ago)

6 **Look at the poster. Fill in the blanks with the correct words below.**

hiking   climbing   horseback riding   fishing   camping

LAURA: I love your poster of New Mexico, Alex.

ALEX: Thanks, Laura. Where would you like to visit?

LAURA: I'd like to visit Taos because ___hiking___ (1)

and _____ (2) are cool!

ALEX: Taos is great, but I like Cochiti.

_____ (3) in the river is great

near Cochiti. _____ (4)

near Cochiti is also fun because the nights

are quiet.

LAURA: Can you ride a horse? How often do you

go _____ (5) near Zuni?

NEW MEXICO

■Taos

Cochiti ■

■Zuni

hike

climb

fish

camp

ride

How + adjective / adverb: questions

How far is Giza from Cairo?   **How long** is the flight to Tokyo?

How old is the Cochiti pueblo?   **How big** are the Pyramids?

---

7 **Fill in the blanks with *How* and *old*, *long*, *far*, *big*, or *good*.**

1 **AYA:** ___How far___ is New Mexico from New York?

ALEX: New York is about 3,200 kilometers from New Mexico.

2 **LAURA:** _____ are the pueblos in New Mexico?

ALEX: A lot of them are 800 or 900 years old.

3 **AYA:** _____ is the fishing in New Mexico?

ALEX: It's fantastic! The rivers are clean.

4 **LAURA:** _____ is New Mexico?

ALEX: It's a big state, but it's smaller than California.

5 **AYA:** _____ is the flight from New Mexico to Tokyo?

ALEX: It's very long. It's 15 hours.

8 🎧 **Listen to the descriptions of the pueblos. Look at the map. Write the pueblo names next to the numbers. Choose from the names below.**

Taos   Santa Clara
Cochiti   Zuni

1 Cochiti

2 _____

3 _____

4 _____

9 **Look at the map again. In your notebooks, write paragraphs about the pueblos.**

Example   Cochiti is the smallest pueblo. There is camping near Cochiti...

10 **Fill in the blanks with the correct forms of the adjectives in parentheses.**

LAURA: Listening to your presentation was fun. It was _____the best_____ presentation this morning.
(**1** *good*)

ALEX: That's not true. Aya's presentation was _____ than mine. Her
(**2** *good*)

presentation was _____ than mine. And her poster was
(**3** *long*)

_____ poster at the conference!
(**4** *big*)

LAURA: Yes, your presentation was a little _____ than hers, and your
(**5** *short*)

poster was _____ than hers, but don't worry! Your presentation
(**6** *small*)

was great!

Put it together!

11 **Make a poster about your country. Use the posters on pages 35 and 37 as models. Include things to do (hiking, camping, swimming, relaxing, etc.) and places to visit (beaches, mountains, famous cities, etc.).**

Rewind — Units 7&8

1 What do they have to do at home? Look at the chart and write sentences. Use *has/have to* or *doesn't/don't have to*.

	Bill	Betty	Chuck and Jim
vacuum the living room			√
cook dinner		√	
wash the car	√	√	

1 <u>Bill and Betty have to wash the car.</u>
  (Bill and Betty / wash)

2 _____
  (Chuck and Jim / cook)

3 _____
  (Betty / vacuum)

4 _____
  (Bill / cook)

5 _____
  (Chuck and Jim / vacuum)

2 Complete the sentences with *might* or *might not* and one of the phrases below.

| hear the telephone | like the dinner | snow | be late | pass the exam |

1 Lucy is running to school. She _____ might be late _____.

2 The music is too loud. We _____.

3 Look at the sky. It _____.

4 Mark and Paul didn't study. They _____.

5 There is a lot of salt in the food. You _____.

3 Read the price list. Label the vegetables in the picture with the correct prices.

VEGETABLE PRICES

Carrots.....$1.80/kilo
Eggplants...$1.10/kilo
Onions......90¢/kilo
Mushrooms...$2.50/kilo
Broccoli....$1.00/kilo
Tomatoes....50¢/kilo
Potatoes....70¢/kilo

$1.10 kilo — 1
kilo — 2
kilo — 3
kilo — 4
kilo — 5
kilo — 6
kilo — 7

4 **Fill in the blanks with the *-ing* form of one of the verbs below.**

climb	sing	live	play	listen	read

1 _____Living_____ in a big city can be exciting.

2 She finished _____ the newspapers an hour ago.

3 _____ mountains is fun, but dangerous.

4 _____ sports is good for you.

5 _____ to the radio is cool.

6 The children love _____ songs.

5 **Complete the questions with *How old*, *How far*, *How big*, and *How long*.**

1 ____How old____ is Petra?   —   She's 14 years old.

2 _____ is the movie?   —   It's two hours.

3 _____ is Rex?   —   He's as big as a lion!

4 _____ is Boston from San Francisco?   —   It's about 4,800 kilometers.

5 _____ is that car?   —   It's 20 years old.

6 **What will happen if you have a party? Write your ideas in your notebook and discuss them with a partner. Then listen to the song.**

If you come to my party,   If you like people and party games,

We'll have a lot of fun.   And music in the sun,

You don't have to bring money.   You should really come to my party.

There's food for old and young!   So put on your sneakers and run!

Unit 9

Clarissa has helped me a lot today.

① 🎧 **Read quickly. Who is the new student? Find out. Then listen.**

SCOTT: Where were you, Clarissa? I was worried about you!

CLARISSA: Sorry, Scott. This is Zoe. Zoe, this is my brother, Scott.

SCOTT: Nice to meet you.

ZOE: Nice to meet you, too. I'm sorry we're late. It's my fault. I'm new here, and your sister has helped me a lot today.

CLARISSA: Zoe's from France!

SCOTT: Oh! I didn't know. You speak English very well, Zoe!

ZOE: My mom is American. I've spoken English all my life.

CLARISSA: Zoe has to get some books. She hasn't studied American history before. We're going to the library.

SCOTT: I'll come with you. I just remembered.... I have to get some books, too.

Got it?

② **Read the conversation again. Answer the questions.**

    1 Why was Scott worried?   —   <u>Because Clarissa was late.</u>

    2 Why was Clarissa late?   —   _____

    3 Why does Zoe speak English well?   —   _____

    4 Why is Scott going to the library?   —   _____

Focus on language!

Present perfect: statements

SUBJECT	+	HAVE/HAS (NOT)	+	PAST PARTICIPLE
I/We/You/They		have (not)		**helped** her a lot today.
He/She/It		has (not)		**taken** a test today.

NOTE: The past participle of regular verbs is the same as the past simple form.

help ┉⟩ help**ed**   study ┉⟩ stud**ied**

The past participle of irregular verbs varies.

be ┉⟩ be**en**   know ┉⟩ know**n**   get ┉⟩ g**otten**

③ Fill in the charts with the missing words.

REGULAR VERBS

Base form	Simple past	Past participle
1 visit	visited	visited
2 cook	_____	cooked
3 dance	_____	danced
4 work	worked	_____
5 play	_____	played

IRREGULAR VERBS

Base form	Simple past	Past participle
6 teach	_____	taught
7 take	took	_____
8 write	_____	written
9 know	knew	_____
10 do	_____	done

④ Fill in the blanks with the present perfect form of the verbs in parentheses. Use the short form.

Tip

Short forms

he has = he**'s**   they have = they**'ve**
he has not = he has**n't**   they have not = they have**n't**

SCOTT: You're going to like this school.

I **'ve learned** _____ a lot of things here.
(**1** *learn*)

Our teachers _____ us a lot.
(**2** *teach*)

ZOE: Great! American history is very difficult for me. I

_____ much history in school.
(**3** *not / study*)

CLARISSA: Scott can help you with that. He _____
(**4** *do*)

well in history this year. He _____ me.
(**5** *help*)

5 Match the school subjects with the pictures.

A B C D E

__ chemistry   A biology   __ art   __ geography   __ physical education

6 Complete the first parts of the sentences with the school subjects in the pictures.

1 Zoe hasn't studied _____ biology _____ this year...

2 Scott has done well in _____ ...

3 Clarissa hasn't done well in _____ ...

4 Scott hasn't enjoyed _____ this year...

5 Zoe and Scott have studied _____ in school...

7 Complete the second parts of the sentences in exercise 6 with the affirmative or negative form of the present perfect.

1 ...but she _____ has studied _____ geography.

2 ...but he _____ well in physical education.

3 ...but she _____ well in art.

4 ...but he _____ biology.

5 ...but they _____ chemistry.

8 **Fill in the blanks with the present perfect or simple past of the verbs in parentheses.**

NEW STUDENT PROFILE

Emory High School Newspaper

Maybe you have _____seen_____ Zoe Millet at school. She is from Lyon, France. She _____moved_____
                    (1 *see***)**   **(2** *move***)**
to Minneapolis in September. She _____ at our school for a month, and she
                                                        (3 *be***)**
_____ herself and _____ many friends. Of course,
              (4 *enjoy***)**   **(5** *make***)**
she _____ very well in French. It's her best subject!
              (6 *do***)**
Last Saturday Zoe _____ to the Mall of America and
                              (7 *go***)**
_____ some fun souvenirs. On Sunday, she _____ the art museum.
      (8 *buy***)**   **(9** *visit***)**

☞ **Tip**

Zoe **has been** to Paris. (We don't know when.)
Use the ***present perfect*** for things that happened at an indefinite time in the past.

Zoe **went** to Paris in 1999. (We know when.)
Use the ***simple past*** for things that happened at a definite time in the past.

9 **Look back at exercise 8 again. Which of the paragraphs below is the best ending for the student profile?**

1 Zoe's parents are French. Her father, Jean Millet, is a scientist. While he was living in France, he worked for a university laboratory. Now he works for a company. Her mother, Anita Millet, is a photographer. She has worked for *All Fashion* magazine.

2 Zoe's father is French, and her mother is American. Her mother has taught her English very well. But Zoe hasn't studied American history before. She studied French history at school in France.

3 Zoe's parents are American. Her father, John Millet, and her mother, Anita Millet, are history teachers. They have worked in many different schools. Zoe has studied American history for many years.

Put it together!

10 **Do you know a new student in your school, or do you have a new friend? In your notebook, write a short profile of him or her. Use exercises 8 and 9 as models.**

Example Carlos is from Barcelona, Spain. He...

Unit 10 Have you ever been in a play?

AROUND THE WORLD IN 80 DAYS

A play from the novel by Jules Verne
October 21 - November 1
King's Theater
All shows at 7:30 P.M.

① 🎧 **Read quickly. What is a *novel*? What is a *play*? Discuss. Then listen.**

SCOTT: Have you seen this play?

ZOE: No, I haven't. I've read the novel. Have you read *Around the World in 80 Days*?

SCOTT: No, I haven't. I don't like novels very much.

ZOE: Have you ever read a novel?

SCOTT: Of course I have! I've read a lot of novels for school, and I've read a Jules Verne novel, too. I read *Journey to the Center of the Earth* last year.... Hey, I have tickets for the play. Clarissa is in it. Would you like to go?

ZOE: Yes, thanks! I'd love to go!

SCOTT: Great! It's going to be exciting. The characters travel to Egypt and India! Have you ever been to India?

ZOE: No. But I've been to Sri Lanka. It's south of India.

Got it?

② **Look at the conversation again. Fill in the blanks with the correct names.**

1 _____Scott_____ hasn't read *Around the World in 80 Days*.

2 _____ doesn't like reading novels.

3 _____ would like to go to the play.

4 _____ is in the play.

Focus on language!

Present perfect: *yes/no* questions and short answers

HAVE	+	SUBJECT	+	PAST PARTICIPLE

yes/no questions

Have	I/you/we/they	seen the play?
Has	he/she/it	done the homework?

short answers

Yes,   I/you/we/they **have.**
      he/she/it **has.**

No,   I/you/we/they **haven't.**
     he/she/it **hasn't.**

---

3 **Answer the questions with short answers.**

1 Have you studied Italian history? — Yes, _____ I have _____.

2 Has she read the novel? — No, _____.

3 Has Scott borrowed any books? — Yes, _____.

4 Have we seen this movie before? — No, _____.

5 Have they cleaned their room? — Yes, _____.

6 Have you been to Australia? — No, _____.

4 **Write the questions. Use the present perfect form of the verbs in parentheses.**

CLARISSA: Has Scott invited you to our play? _____
(**1** *Scott / invite you to our play*)

ZOE: Yes, he has.

CLARISSA: Great! _____
(**2** *you / see this play before*)

ZOE: No, I haven't.

CLARISSA: _____
(**3** *you / read the novel*)

ZOE: Yes, I have. I loved it, and I loved the movie!

_____
(**4** *you / see the movie*)

CLARISSA: No, I haven't.

Present perfect: *ever* and *never*

HAVE	+	SUBJECT	+	EVER	+	PAST PARTICIPLE
Have		you		ever		**been** to France?
Has		he		ever		**read** a novel?

questions

answers

Yes, I have been to France. / **No,** I have **never** been to France.

Yes, he has read a novel. / **No,** he has **never** read a novel.

Note: Short forms = I've been... / I've never been...

5 **Make questions. Use the words in parentheses.**

1 <u>Have you ever been to Sri Lanka?</u>

             (you / ever / be / Sri Lanka)

2 _____

             (your teacher / ever / be / on TV)

3 _____

             (your friends / ever / study German)

4 _____

             (your national soccer team / ever / win the World Cup)

5 _____

             (you / ever / see / an elephant)

6 _____

             (you / ever / use / a computer)

6 **Answer the questions in exercise 5 with true information. Use long answers.**

1 <u>Yes, I have been to Sri Lanka.</u> *or* <u>No, I have never been to Sri Lanka.</u>

2 _____

3 _____

4 _____

5 _____

6 _____

7 🎧 **Listen to the dialog. Check the correct boxes.**

	ZOE	CLARISSA	SCOTT
has never acted in a play	✓		
has seen a lot of plays	✓		
has been to Egypt			
has been to Greece			

8 **Look at the map. Fill in the blanks with *north*, *south*, *east*, or *west*.**

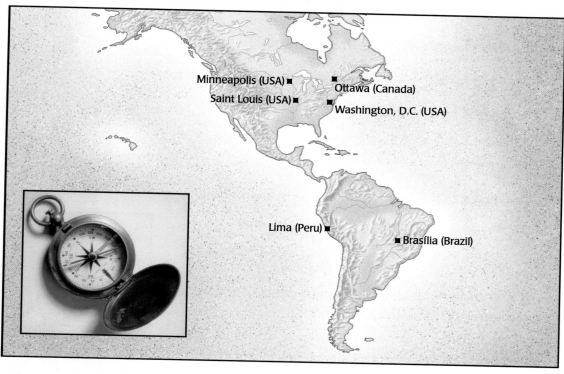

1 Lima is ___south___ of Washington, D.C.

2 Brasília is _____ of Lima.

3 Saint Louis is _____ of Washington, D.C.

4 Ottawa is _____ of Washington, D.C.

5 Minneapolis is _____ of Ottawa.

9 **Answer the questions. Use other places and the direction words from exercise 8.**

1 Where is New York? — It's north of Washington, D.C. _____

2 Where is your city? — _____

3 Where is your state? — _____

4 Where is your country? — _____

Put it together!

10 **Write a paragraph about the places you have been to and when you were there.**

Example I have never been to another country, but I have been to other cities in my country. I have been to... . I went there in 2000. I have also been to... . It's north of... . I went there last year.

Rewind — Units 9 & 10

1 Fill in the blanks with the correct letters.

Base form	Simple past	Past participle
1 c _o_ me	came	c _o_ me
2 get	g __ t	g __ tt __ __
3 g __	w __ __ __	gone
4 kn __ w	knew	kn __ w __
5 m __ __ t	met	met
6 speak	sp __ k __	spoken

2 Fill in the blanks with the present perfect of the verbs in parentheses. Use the short forms.

My name's Judy Smith. I' _ve done_____ a lot of interesting
     (1 do)

things in my life, and I _____ a lot of
              (2 visit)

countries. My husband _____ a lot of
              (3 do)

interesting things, too, but he _____ to
              (4 not / be)

many countries. I _____ at Carnival in Brazil, and
          (5 dance)

I _____ the Pyramids in Egypt. I _____ to India, but my
   (6 see)   **(7 not / be)**

husband and I will go there next year. We _____ together before!
                          (8 not / travel)

3 What were Judy's favorite subjects? Fill in the blanks with the words below.

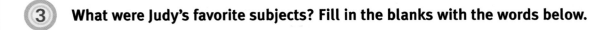

| art | biology | geography | physical education |

I've always loved to learn about other countries. At school, I learned about artists from other

countries in my _____art_____ classes. I used to ask my _____ teacher
           (1)   **(2)**

questions about the rivers, the mountains, and the population of each country, and my

_____ teacher taught me about animals and plants. But I also loved
     (3)

sports. My _____ teacher used to run races all over the world.
       (4)

49

④ Complete the chart with your answers (✓ = *yes* and X = *no*). Then complete the questions and answers.

HAVE YOU EVER...	TERRY	JENNY	YOU
written a song?	X	✓	
won a race?	✓	✓	
seen a snake?	✓	X	

1 <u>Has Terry ever seen a snake?</u>   —   <u>Yes, he has.</u>
        (Terry / snake)

2 _____   —   _____
        (Jenny / snake)

3 _____   —   _____
        (you / song)

4 _____   —   _____
        (Terry and Jenny / race)

⑤ Fill in the blanks with the present perfect or simple past of the verbs in parentheses.

ANDY: _<u>Have</u>_ you ever _<u>been</u>_ (**1** *be*) to the cities near Washington, D.C.?

BEN: Yes! I _____ (**2** *visit*) Colesville. And I _____

(**3** *go*) to North Potomac last week.

ANDY: Colesville is north of Washington. But where is North Potomac?

BEN: North Potomac is west of Colesville.

ANDY: Oh. I _____ (**4** *travel*) to Fort Hunt. It's south of Washington.

BEN: Fort Hunt is east of Manassas. _____ you ever _____ (**5** *be*)

to Manassas? It's great!

⑥ Look at exercise 5. Then match the names of the cities and the numbers on the map.

<u>2</u> Colesville

— Fort Hunt

— Manassas

— North Potomac

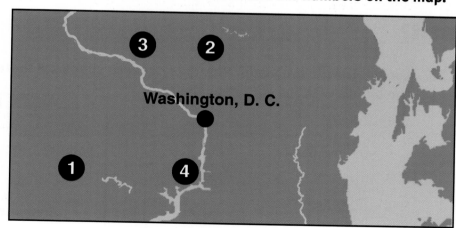

Unit 11 — She hasn't seen her since 1981!

1 🎧 **Read quickly. What is a *heart*? Circle the correct answer. Then listen.**

a color   **b** shape   **c** balloon

SCOTT:	How long have you been in here?
CLARISSA:	I've been in here for an hour.
SCOTT:	What are you painting?
CLARISSA:	It's the balloon for the play. The actors are going to travel around the world in it!
SCOTT:	It looks great. I like the hearts.
CLARISSA:	Thanks. I'm going to paint some shapes around here next. What's Mom doing?
SCOTT:	She's on the phone.
CLARISSA:	She's been on the phone for a long time!
SCOTT:	I know. She's talking to a friend from her university. She hasn't seen her since 1981!

Got it?

2 **Look at the picture again. How many of each shape are there on the balloon? Fill in the blanks with the correct numbers.**

1 _0_ stars   **5** __ rectangles

2 __ diamonds   **6** __ triangles

3 __ hearts   **7** __ squares

4 __ circles

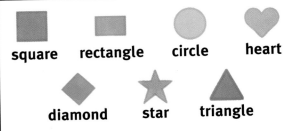

square   rectangle   circle   heart

diamond   star   triangle

Focus on language!

Present perfect: *since* and *for*

SINCE + A SPECIFIC POINT IN TIME	FOR + LENGTH/PERIOD OF TIME
Mom has been on the phone **since** eight o'clock.	Mom has been on the phone **for** three hours.
We've lived in Minneapolis **since** September.	We've lived in Minneapolis **for** a month.

Use *since* or *for* and the present perfect to talk about something that began in the past and continues until now.

3 Fill in the blanks with *since* or *for*.

1 ___for___ a year

2 ___since___ 9:30

3 _____ six hours

4 _____ August 9th

5 _____ 1998

6 _____ last night

7 _____ this morning

8 _____ four months

9 _____ 5 o'clock

10 _____ ten days

11 _____ a long time

12 _____ two minutes

4 Fill in the blanks with *since* or *for*.

MOM: Scott, I need to talk to you ___for___ a minute. My friend's daughter would like to
(1)

go to Clarissa's play with you. We discussed this...don't you remember?

SCOTT: Oh, no! I forgot! Mom, I've invited a

new friend to the play. I've had these

plans _____ a few days..._____
(2)   (3)

last Tuesday!

MOM: Please, Scott. It will only be _____ a
(4)

few hours! This girl hasn't been in

Minneapolis _____ very long. I
(5)

promised my friend! And I haven't seen

her _____ 1981!
(6)

(5) **Write sentences using the words in parentheses. Use the present perfect with**
since or *for.*

1 <u>Mom has been on the phone since 5:30.</u>
                    (Mom / be on the phone / 5:30)

2 _____
           (The girl / not / live in Minneapolis / a long time)

3 _____
           (Clarissa and Scott / know Zoe / last Monday)

4 _____
           (Clarissa / study Spanish / three years)

5 _____
           (We / not / see them / 1999)

Present perfect: information questions

QUESTION WORD	+	*HAVE*	+	SUBJECT	+	PAST PARTICIPLE
Who		have		you		invited to the play?
Where		have		they		gone?
What		has		she		done?
How long		have		I		known her?

(6) **Write information questions with the words in parentheses and the present perfect.**

1 <u>Where have you been?</u>
              (Where / you / be)

2 _____
           (Who / Scott / invite to the play)

3 _____
           (How long / her friends / live here)

4 _____
           (What / Clarissa / paint)

5 _____
           (How many colors / she / use in her painting)

(7) **Fill in the blanks with a question word and *since* or *for.***

1 <u>How long</u> has Zoe lived in Minneapolis?   — <u>For</u> one month.

2 _____ has Mrs. Vermont worked _____ 1997? — At the school.

3 _____ has Clarissa done _____ September 1st? — She's practiced for her play.

4 _____ has waited for Clarissa _____ an hour? — Clarissa's mother.

8 **Read the dialog. Look at the underlined words in the answers. Write the questions.**

SCOTT: What am I going to do? Should I take that girl to the play? Mom has known this family for a long time.

CLARISSA: Yes, and they've been in Minneapolis for only a few weeks. This girl probably doesn't have any friends here. She'll be disappointed if she can't go to the play with you.

SCOTT: But I've invited Zoe! She might be angry if I don't go with her! She might never talk to me again!

1 How long has Mom known this family? _____

Mom has known this family <u>for a long time</u>.

2 _____

The family has been in town <u>for only a few weeks</u>.

3 _____

<u>Scott</u> has invited Zoe to the play.

4 _____

Zoe <u>might never talk to Scott again</u> if he doesn't go with her.

9 **What should Scott do? Should he take Zoe to the play? Should he take the other girl? Discuss your opinion in pairs.**

Examples STUDENT A: I think he should take Zoe. He's had those plans for days.

STUDENT B: I think he should take the other girl because she probably doesn't have any friends in Minneapolis.

Put it together!

10 **Have you ever had a problem like Scott's? What did you do? Write about it in your notebook.**

Example Yes, I've had a problem like Scott's. Last month I invited a friend to a movie. Then my mother planned a visit to my grandmother's house on the same day. I went to my grandmother's house, and my friend and I went to the movie on a different day.

Unit 12

I haven't met her yet.

THEATER REVIEW

80 Days and Five Countries in Two Hours!

The new production of *Around the World in 80 Days* at the King's Theater is excellent. The actors are wonderful. The sets are colorful, and the story is really exciting! Opening night for the public is tomorrow. Take your friends and family!

1 🎧 **Read quickly. Is Scott going to take Zoe to the play? Find the answer. Then listen.**

ZOE: Scott! I've just read the review of Clarissa's play! Have you seen it yet?

SCOTT: I've already seen the review. I read it this morning.

ZOE: What's the matter?

SCOTT: Zoe, I have to tell you something. I can't take you to the play tomorrow. I have to take the daughter of my mother's friend.

ZOE: But, Scott...

SCOTT: I'm sorry, Zoe. I don't want to disappoint you, but I have to do this for my mother. Let's go to a movie at the Rialto on Saturday.

ZOE: OK. But...

SCOTT: I'll see you later!

Got it?

2 **Look at exercise 1. Where can you find the information? Write *TR* for *theater review* or *C* for *conversation*.**

1 Clarissa is in the play.   C

2 The play is at King's Theater.   ___

3 Opening night is tomorrow.   ___

4 There's a movie at the Rialto on Saturday.   ___

Focus on language!

Present perfect: *already* and *yet*

Have they **opened** the theater **yet**? — Yes, they **have already opened** the theater.
— No, they **haven't opened** the theater **yet**.

Use *already* in affirmative statements. It is usually between *have* and the past participle.

Use *yet* in questions and negative statements. It is always at the end of a sentence.

3 Circle the correct words in parentheses.

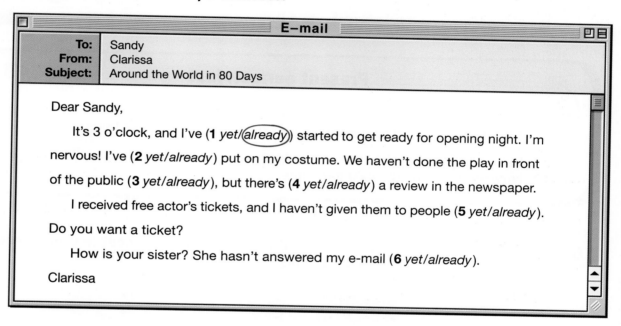

E-mail

To:	Sandy
From:	Clarissa
Subject:	Around the World in 80 Days

Dear Sandy,

It's 3 o'clock, and I've (**1** *yet*/*already*) started to get ready for opening night. I'm nervous! I've (**2** *yet*/*already*) put on my costume. We haven't done the play in front of the public (**3** *yet*/*already*), but there's (**4** *yet*/*already*) a review in the newspaper.

I received free actor's tickets, and I haven't given them to people (**5** *yet*/*already*). Do you want a ticket?

How is your sister? She hasn't answered my e-mail (**6** *yet*/*already*).

Clarissa

4 Look at Clarissa's checklist. Answer the questions. Use *yet* or *already*.

1 Has Clarissa painted the balloon for the play yet?
   Yes, she has already painted the balloon for the play.

2 Has she written an e-mail to Sandy yet?
   _____

3 Has she called Aunt Betty yet?
   _____

4 Has she read the review of the play yet?
   _____

5 Has she taken a shower yet?
   _____

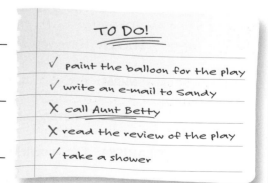

TO DO!

✓ paint the balloon for the play
✓ write an e-mail to Sandy
✗ call Aunt Betty
✗ read the review of the play
✓ take a shower

5 **Look at the picture. It's 8 P.M. Match the verbs with the people in the house.**

1 answer the phone <u>C</u>   **2** put away __   **3** turn on __   **4** turn off __

Present perfect: *just*

Clarissa was not ready a moment ago. She **has just put on** her costume.
The theater was closed a moment ago. They **have just opened** the doors.

Use *just* to show that something happened a moment ago. It is usually between *have* and the past participle.

6 **Look at the picture again. Now it's 8:01. What has just happened? In your notebook, write sentences about the people using the verbs in the box.**

answer the phone	**turn off the TV**
turn on the coffee machine	**put away the food**

Example   Clarissa has just answered the phone.

7 **Now it's 8:30. Complete the conversation with *just*, *already*, or *yet*.**

CLARISSA: That girl has ___just___ arrived in a car!
(1)

SCOTT: Have you seen her _____? Is she pretty?
(2)

MOM: I've _____ told you ten times, Scott. She's a beautiful girl.
(3)

SCOTT: I haven't seen her _____, but she can't be as pretty as Zoe.
(4)

CLARISSA: Oh, wow! Don't say that _____! I can see her now.... She's _____
(5)   (6)

gotten out of the car! I think you've met her _____!
(7)

8 Fill in the blanks with the simple past or present perfect of the verbs in parentheses.

SCOTT: <u>Have</u> you <u>had</u> (**1** *have*) dinner yet?

ZOE: No, I haven't.

SCOTT: Cool! Let's eat after the play.... I can't believe you're Mom's friend's daughter! But you _____ (**2** *know*) about this yesterday, and you _____ (**3** *not / tell*) me! Why?

ZOE: Because you _____ (**4** *not / give*) me time yesterday.

SCOTT: That's true...but how long _____ you _____ (**5** *know*)?

ZOE: I _____ (**6** *know*) since last Thursday. _____ you _____ (**7** *be*) worried for two days?

SCOTT: Well, a little. But I _____ (**8** *be*) very surprised when I _____ (**9** *see*) you at the door an hour ago! And I _____ (**10** *be*) very happy, too!

9 Read the conversation again. Answer the questions.

1 Has Zoe had dinner yet? — <u>No, she hasn't.</u>

2 How long has Zoe known about Scott's mom? — _____

3 Has Scott been worried for two days? — _____

4 When was Scott surprised? — _____

5 Why was Scott happy? — _____

Put it together!

10 What have you already done today? What haven't you done yet? What have you just done? Write sentences in your notebook.

Examples I've already taken a shower.

I haven't watched TV yet.

I've just come to English class.

Rewind — Units 11&12

1 Put the time expressions in the correct group.

| 20 years | an hour | 1981 | a long time | 9 o'clock | 8:30 |
| November | fifteen minutes | last Monday | a few days |

for: ____20 years____ _____ _____ _____ _____

since: ____1981____ _____ _____ _____ _____

2 Look at the underlined parts of the answers. Write questions.

1 Why has she made a cake?___ — Because <u>Jan has invited her to a party</u>.

2 _____ — I've been <u>at the library</u>.

3 _____ — <u>Robert</u> has seen this movie.

4 _____ — Thomas has <u>written a letter</u>.

5 _____ — I've gone to bed <u>because I'm tired</u>.

3 Write questions with *How long*.

1 Sue works in a bank. — How long has she worked there?___

2 I live in Chicago. — _____

3 Sara knows Mark. — _____

4 We are doctors. — _____

5 John works in China. — _____

4 Fill in the blanks with the correct shapes.

1 The ____square____ is yellow.

2 The _____ is red.

3 The _____ is pink.

4 The _____ is green.

5 The _____ is orange.

6 The _____ is blue.

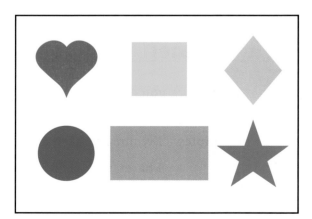

5 Look at the picture. Lucy is packing her bag for a trip. Write sentences using *yet* and *already*.

1 <u>She hasn't packed her slippers yet.</u>

2 <u>She has already packed her shoes.</u>

3 _____

4 _____

5 _____

6 _____

6 What has just happened? Complete the sentences using *just* and the words below.

> take a shower   eat the fish   wake up   cook the fish

1

The girl _____ has just cooked the fish. _____

The cat _____ .

2

The baby _____ .

The mother _____ .

7 🎧 Listen to the song and fill in the blanks.

Hey, people, ___have___ you heard the news?
(1)
Big Bob is back in town!

I haven't seen him _____, it's true,
(2)
But I know that he's around.

He's been away _____ seven years.
(3)
If you ask where, he'll smile.

I haven't seen Big Bob 'round here

_____ I was a child.
(4)

Big Bob, Big Bob...he's always been a mystery.

Big Bob, Big Bob...the biggest Bob in history.

Unit 13

You're Rose's friend, aren't you?

1 🎧 **Read quickly. Find out why Shelley doesn't recognize Riccardo. Then listen.**

RICCARDO: Hi, Shelley, right? You're Rose's friend, aren't you?

SHELLEY: Yes, I am. Umm...do I know you?

RICCARDO: We met at a swimming competition last year. You were the fastest swimmer on Rose's team, weren't you?

SHELLEY: Yes, I was, but I'm sorry...I don't remember you.

RICCARDO: I'm Riccardo. I'm Rose's cousin, from Italy.

SHELLEY: Riccardo! I didn't recognize you! You look different!

RICCARDO: I've grown a lot.

SHELLEY: Yes, you have. Hey! Something smells great!

RICCARDO: Rose is making hamburgers in the backyard.

Got it?

2 **Read the conversation again. Write short answers.**

1 Are Rose and Shelley friends? — <u>Yes, they are.</u>

2 Was Shelley the fastest swimmer on the team last year? — _____

3 Are Riccardo and Shelley cousins? — _____

4 Is Riccardo shorter than last year? — _____

5 Is Rose in the backyard? — _____

61

Focus on language!

Tag questions: simple present of *be*

AFFIRMATIVE SENTENCE	NEGATIVE TAG	NEGATIVE SENTENCE	AFFIRMATIVE TAG
I **am** very late,	**aren't** I?	I **am** not late,	**am** I?
He **is** very late,	**isn't** he?	She **is** not late,	**is** she?
We **are** very late,	**aren't** we?	They **are** not late,	**are** they?

3 Fill in the blanks with the correct form of the verb *be*.

1 You're Rose's cousin, _____aren't_____ you?   —   Yes, I ____am____ .

2 I'm a lot taller now, _____ I?   —   Yes, you _____ .

3 Shelley is not a bad swimmer, _____ she?   —   No, she _____ .

4 Rose and her family aren't in the kitchen,

_____ they?   —   No, they _____ .

5 It's a beautiful day, _____ it?   —   Yes, it _____ .

6 Riccardo is not from Spain, _____ he?   —   No, he _____ .

4 Read the conversation. Fill in the blanks with the correct tag questions.

MRS. LUTZ: Shelley! You're here! You're a little late, ____aren't you____ ?
(1)

SHELLEY: Yes, I am. Sorry. I was talking to Riccardo.

MRS. LUTZ: That's OK. ... Rose! This hamburger is for

Shelley, _____ ?
(2)

ROSE: Yes, it is, Mom.... Hey, Riccardo's really

different, _____ ?
(3)

SHELLEY: Yes, he is. I didn't recognize him!

He isn't a little boy anymore,

_____ ?
(4)

ROSE: No, he isn't! And he's really nice,

_____ ?
(5)

SHELLEY: Yes, he is. He's very kind. He remembered

me from last year.

Tag questions: simple past of *be*

AFFIRMATIVE SENTENCE	NEGATIVE TAG	NEGATIVE SENTENCE	AFFIRMATIVE TAG
I **was** there,	**wasn't** I?	I **wasn't** there,	**was** I?
They **were** hungry,	**weren't** they?	They **weren't** hungry,	**were** they?

5 **Fill in the blanks with the correct form of the verb *be*.**

1 You __were__ at the party yesterday, weren't you?   —   Yes, I __was__.

2 He _____ in Italy last week, was he?   —   No, he _____.

3 We _____ in the kitchen a minute ago, weren't we?   —   Yes, we _____.

4 That _____ Rose's hamburger, was it?   —   No, it _____.

5 The glasses _____ on the table, weren't they?   —   Yes, they _____.

6 **Match the sentences and the tag questions.**

1 Riccardo is from Italy,   A is she?
2 The hamburgers were great,   B aren't they?
3 Shelley and Rose are best friends,   C was it?
4 The food wasn't terrible,   D isn't he?
5 Mrs. Lutz isn't Shelley's aunt, E weren't they?

7 **Look at the pictures. Fill in the blanks with the verbs below.**

  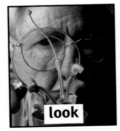  

smell   **taste**   **look**   **feel**   **sound**

1 This song __sounds__ beautiful.

2 She's cooking some fish right now. It _____ great!

3 You _____ wonderful in that dress.

4 Can I have more french fries? They _____ delicious.

5 The water is freezing.

   It _____ so cold!

> **Tip**
>
> The music sounds **good**.   The soup smells/tastes **great**.
> She looks **beautiful**.   The dress feels **soft**.
> When these verbs refer to a state (how something is),
> they are followed by adjectives.

8 **Fill in the blanks with the verbs from exercise 7.**

SHELLEY: Has your mom just baked cookies? They ___smell___ good!
(1)

ROSE: Would you like some? Here!

SHELLEY: Ouch! They _____ hot!... But they _____
(2)   (3)

delicious!

MRS. LUTZ: Thanks! Shelley, I like your new haircut. It _____ pretty!
(4)

SHELLEY: Thanks!... Hey! Who's singing?

ROSE: That's Riccardo. Doesn't his voice _____ good?
(5)

He's in a band in Italy!

9 **Listen to the conversation. Circle _T_ (_True_) or _F_ (_False_).**

1 Rose was in Italy three years ago.   T / F
2 Rose's aunt and uncle are not going to visit her.   T / F
3 Riccardo is going to Italy in three weeks.   T / F
4 Rose will come back to the United States next summer.   T / F
5 Shelley knew about Rose's plans.   T / F

10 **Discuss the conversation in exercise 9 with a partner. Should Shelley be so angry and unhappy? What do you think?**

Example Shelley shouldn't be angry because Rose has to be with her family.

Put it together!

11 **Have any of your friends or relatives moved to another city or country? How did you feel? Did you miss the person? Write a paragraph about it in your notebook.**

Example My friend Marco moved to Los Angeles last year. I missed him a lot...

Unit 14 You still like me, don't you?

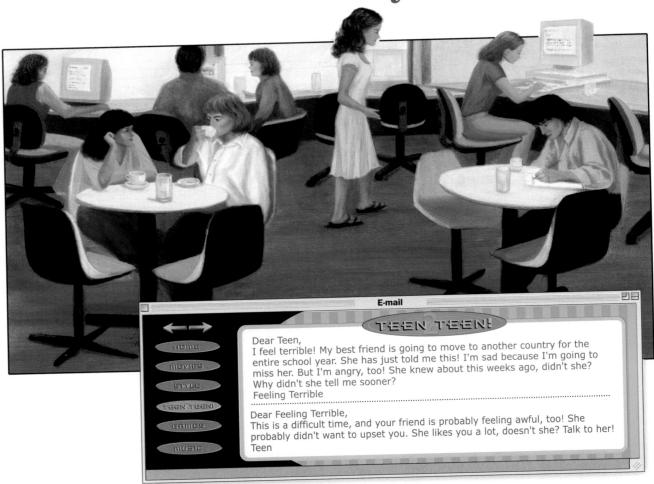

E-mail

TEEN 2 TEEN!

Dear Teen,
I feel terrible! My best friend is going to move to another country for the entire school year. She has just told me this! I'm sad because I'm going to miss her. But I'm angry, too! She knew about this weeks ago, didn't she? Why didn't she tell me sooner?
Feeling Terrible
....
Dear Feeling Terrible,
This is a difficult time, and your friend is probably feeling awful, too! She probably didn't want to upset you. She likes you a lot, doesn't she? Talk to her!
Teen

HOME
MOVIES
STYLE
TEEN TEEN!
GAMES
MUSIC

① 🎧 **Read the Web page quickly. Who wrote the e-mail to Teen? Guess. Then listen.**

Tip

I feel **terrible**.
I feel **cold**.

Use *feel* to talk about emotions and physical conditions.

Got it?

② **Read the web page again. Where did you find the information? Write *E* for *e-mail*. Write *A* for Teen's answer.**

1 Feeling Terrible's best friend is going away for the school year. __E__

2 The best friend probably feels awful, too. __—__

3 Feeling Terrible should talk to her best friend. __—__

4 Feeling Terrible feels sad and angry. __—__

Focus on language!

Tag questions: simple present

AFFIRMATIVE SENTENCE	NEGATIVE TAG	NEGATIVE SENTENCE	AFFIRMATIVE TAG
I travel a lot,	don't I?	You don't travel a lot,	do you?
He travels a lot,	doesn't he?	She doesn't travel a lot,	does she?

3 Fill in the blanks with the correct words.

1 Rose likes Shelley, __doesn't__ she?   — Yes, she __does__ .

2 Shelley feels terrible, _____ she?   — Yes, she _____ .

3 Riccardo doesn't speak French, _____ he?   — No, he _____ .

4 *Teen 2 Teen!* helps a lot of teens, _____ it?   — Yes, it _____ .

5 Your parents don't live in Cuba, _____ they?   — No, they _____ .

6 You and Rose don't swim on a team, _____ you? — No, we _____ .

4 Read the conversation. Fill in the blanks with the correct tag questions.

ROSE: Hi, Shelley. We haven't talked for four days. You still like me, __don't you__ ?
(1)

SHELLEY: Yes, I do, but I don't want to talk right now. You know why, _____ ?
(2)

ROSE: Yes, I do. I feel bad. Riccardo feels terrible, too. He really likes you! You don't dislike him, _____ ?
(3)

SHELLEY: No, of course I don't. Your flight leaves in ten days, _____ ?
(4)

ROSE: Yes, it does. Why don't we go to the pool? You still like swimming, _____ ?
(5)

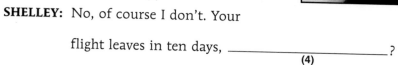

66

⑤ Look at the pictures. Fill in the blanks with the correct words.

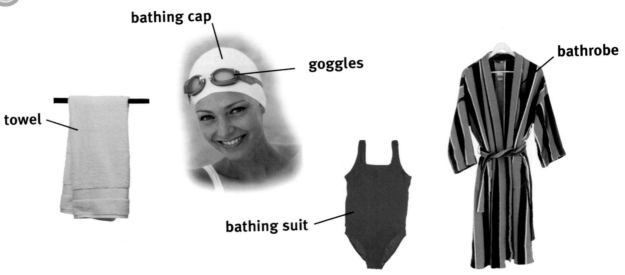

bathing cap

goggles

bathrobe

towel

bathing suit

1 She is wearing a _____bathing cap_____ on her head.

2 She has _____. She can see easily while she is swimming.

3 It was cold. He put on his _____.

4 His hair is wet! He needs a _____.

5 She usually wears a purple _____ at the pool.

Tag questions: simple past

AFFIRMATIVE SENTENCE	NEGATIVE TAG	NEGATIVE SENTENCE	AFFIRMATIVE TAG
You **went** to the pool,	**didn't** you?	I **didn't go** to the pool,	**did** I?
She **went** to the pool,	**didn't** she?	He **didn't go** to the pool,	**did** he?

⑥ Write sentences with the simple past and tag questions.

1 The kids went swimming yesterday, didn't they?
  (The kids / go swimming / yesterday)

2 _____
  (Shelley / write to Teen / last night)

3 _____
  (Rose / not go to the cafe / last week)

4 _____
  (Rose / not use her goggles / today)

5 _____
  (Riccardo / not take a bathrobe / to the pool)

6 _____
  (Shelley / read Teen's answer / this morning)

(7) Fill in the blanks with the correct words.

ROSE: I've had these plans for two months.

I'm sorry. You're still angry,

<u>aren't you</u> ?
(1)

SHELLEY: Yes, a little.

ROSE: These plans surprised you,

_____?
(2)

SHELLEY: Yes, they did! We're friends,

_____? We
(3)

always share our problems,

_____?
(4)

ROSE: You're right. I feel awful, and I'm scared! My Italian isn't very good. And I don't

have any friends there, _____?
(5)

SHELLEY: Wow. I'm sorry, Rose. This isn't easy for you, _____?
(6)

(8) Look at exercise 7. Write *T* (*True*) or *F* (*False*) beside the sentences below.

1 Rose has just made her plans to go to Italy. <u>F</u>

2 Shelley is still a little angry. ___

3 Rose and Shelley never share their problems. ___

4 Rose is thrilled about going to Italy. ___

(9) In your notebook, rewrite the false sentences from exercise 8 as true sentences.

Example Rose made her plans to go to Italy two months ago.

Put it together!

(10) How much do you know about your friends? Write true information about a partner in your notebook. Then check your information with tag questions.

Example **STUDENT A:** You like chocolate, don't you?
STUDENT B: Yes, I do!

Rewind — Units 13 &14

1 Match the pictures (A-D) with the questions (1-4).

A

C

B

D

1 "They aren't happy, are they?" C

2 "He's handsome, isn't he?" —

3 "You were hungry, weren't you?" —

4 "We weren't very good, were we?" —

2 Write answers to the questions above.

1 " No, they aren't."

2 "_____."

3 "_____."

4 "_____."

3 Fill in the blanks with the correct pronoun and the verb *be*. Use the short forms.

1 ___They're___ your parents, aren't they?

2 _____ Mark's girlfriend, was she?

3 _____ a fast swimmer, are you?

4 _____ at school yesterday, was I?

5 _____ good friends, aren't we?

6 _____ a very nice day, is it?

4 Fill in the blanks with the correct tag questions.

1 This soup tastes great, _____ doesn't it _____ ?

2 I didn't show you my homework, _____ ?

3 Susan went to the movies last night, _____ ?

4 He doesn't look good in that coat, _____ ?

5 Maria's cookies smelled great, _____ ?

6 This guitar doesn't sound good, _____ ?

5 Fill in the blanks with the correct verb forms.

WOMAN: Excuse me. You're John Dyer, _____ aren't _____ you?
(1)

MAN: Yes, I _____ .
(2)

WOMAN: You went to Tadville High School, _____ you?
(3)

MAN: Yes, I _____ .
(4)

WOMAN: And you remember Mrs. Stein, _____ you?
(5)

MAN: Oh, yes, I _____ . She was an Olympic
(6)

swimmer, _____ she?
(7)

WOMAN: Yes, she _____ .
(8)

MAN: Ah, I remember you now! You're Mrs. Stein's daughter. Your name is Emily,

_____ it?
(9)

WOMAN: Er...no, it _____ . It's Emma.
(10)

6 Fill in the missing letters in the "swimming words" to discover the mystery word.

```
B _ T H _ N G      C _ _
               T _ W _ _
            _ A T _ R _ B _
            G O _ _ _ E S
```

Mystery word = _____

Unit 15

It's a document that shows your country.

1 🎧 **Read quickly. Find the thing that travelers need. Then listen.**

ROSE: Hey, Shelley, your little brother has taken my passport!

SHELLEY: Stevie, give Rose her passport!

STEVIE: OK. But what's a passport?

ROSE: It's a document that shows your country. A traveler needs it.

STEVIE: What's a traveler?

SHELLEY: It's a person who goes on a trip.

STEVIE: Oh.... What's this big book?

ROSE: It's our family photo album.

SHELLEY: Cool! This album has pictures of your relatives in Italy, doesn't it? Can we look at them?

Got it?

2 **Read the conversation again. Answer the questions.**

1 What has Stevie done? — <u>He's taken Rose's passport.</u>

2 Who needs passports? — _____

3 What's the big book? — _____

4 Who is in the pictures in the photo album? — _____

Focus on language!

Relative clauses with *who*

singular

A stuntman is a person. A stuntman does dangerous things for actors.
A stuntman is a person **who** does dangerous things for actors.

plural

My parents are those people. They are sitting by the door.
My parents are those people **who** are sitting by the door.

3 Give definitions of the occupations. Use relative clauses.

1 A flight attendant is a person who works on a plane.
(flight attendant / works on a plane)

2 _____
(photographer / takes pictures)

3 _____
(teacher / teaches people)

4 _____
(tourist / visits other places)

5 _____
(mechanics / fix cars)

6 _____
(hairdressers / cut hair)

4 Look at the picture of Rose's relatives in Italy. In your notebook, rewrite the sentences below using relative clauses.

Example That's Rose's uncle Eduardo. He's wearing shorts.

Rose's uncle Eduardo is the man who is wearing shorts.

1 That's Rose's grandfather. He has white hair.
2 That's Rose's aunt Alice. She's wearing a blue dress.
3 That's Rose's cousin Bianca. She's three years old.
4 That's Rose's grandmother. She's sitting behind Eduardo.

Relative clauses with *that*

singular

A passport is a document. A passport shows your country.
　A passport is a document **that** shows your country.

plural

Suitcases are things. Suitcases carry clothes.
　Suitcases are things **that** carry clothes.

5 Match pictures 1–4 with A–D.

1

A holds money

3

B cuts meat

2

C makes music

4

D carries clothes

6 Look at exercise 5 again. In your notebook, write sentences about the objects. Use relative clauses.

Example　A suitcase is a thing that carries clothes.

7 Study the picture and the key. Then put the words in the key in the correct columns.

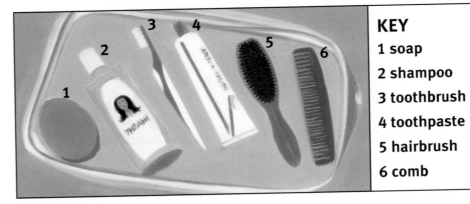

KEY

1 soap
2 shampoo
3 toothbrush
4 toothpaste
5 hairbrush
6 comb

For teeth

toothpaste

For taking a shower

For hair

8 **Fill in the blanks with words from exercise 7. Use plural forms where needed.**

1 A _____toothbrush_____ is a brush that cleans your teeth.

2 _____ is a paste that cleans your teeth.

3 A _____ is a thing that brushes hair.

4 _____ are liquids that clean hair.

5 _____ is a thing that cleans and washes.

6 _____ are things that comb hair.

9 **Fill in the blanks with *who* or *that*.**

1 A joystick is a thing __that__ controls a computer game.

2 Teenagers are people _____ are older than 12 and younger than 20.

3 Subways are trains _____ move people under the ground.

4 A cup is an object _____ holds coffee.

5 Students are people _____ go to school.

10 **Look at the photographs. Listen to the dialog. Then write the correct names under the pictures.**

Francesca   **Aldo**   **Piero**

1    2    3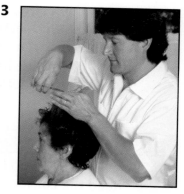

_____Francesca_____   _____   _____

Put it together!

11 **In your notebook, draw or paste a picture of your family, your friends, or a group of people. Describe the people. Use relative clauses.**

Example   Carlos is the boy who is holding a camera. Lisa is the girl who is wearing a pink T-shirt...

Unit 16

There's a surprise party for Rose!

① 🎧 **Read quickly. What does Riccardo say about his English? Then listen.**

RICCARDO: Thanks for helping me with Rose's surprise party, Shelley. I don't know this city very well, and my English is not very good.

SHELLEY: That's not true. You speak English very well!

RICCARDO: Thank you. My grammar is good, but sometimes my vocabulary isn't very good. I don't know the names of some things. For example, the place where you buy bread and cakes...what do you call it?

SHELLEY: A bakery.

RICCARDO: Oh, yes, I remember now! A bakery is a place where you buy bread and cakes. We have to go to the bakery. I'm going to buy a cake for Rose.

SHELLEY: Great! Let's take the bus to the city.

Got it?

② **Read the conversation again. Match the beginnings (1–4) and the ends (A–D) of the sentences.**

1 Riccardo doesn't
2 Shelley is helping
3 They are going to take
4 They are going to buy

A the bus to the city.
B know the city very well.
C Riccardo with the party.
D a cake at the bakery.

③ **Which is easier for you: English grammar or vocabulary? Discuss your opinion in groups.**

Example   I think English vocabulary is easier because I listen to many songs in English.

Focus on language!

Relative clauses with *where*

A post office is a place. You buy stamps at the post office.
A post office is a place **where** you buy stamps.

We are going to the beach. They sell ice cream at the beach.
We are going to the beach **where** they sell ice cream.

4 **Write sentences with *a place* and a relative clause, using the words in parentheses.**

1 <u>A kitchen is a place where you cook food.</u>
(kitchen / cook food)

2 _____
(shopping mall / go shopping)

3 _____
(theater / see a play)

4 _____
(supermarket / buy food)

5 _____
(bank / put money)

5 **Play a game. Think of a place. Say a clue. Your classmate guesses the place.**

Example **STUDENT A:** This is a place where you learn a lot of things.

STUDENT B: A school!

6 **Combine the sentence pairs into one sentence with a relative clause.**

1 I'm going to the store. They sell my favorite candy at the store.

<u>I'm going to the store where they sell my favorite candy.</u>

2 She always waits at the bus stop. Bus number 6 stops at the bus stop.

_____

3 They went to the theater. My sister works at the theater.

_____

4 We ate at the Mexican restaurant. The food is delicious at the restaurant.

_____

5 He visited the city. There are famous buildings in the city.

_____

7 Look at the picture. Fill in the blanks with the correct words.

1 A _____drugstore_____ is a place where you can buy shampoo and toothpaste.

2 A _____ is a place where you put gasoline in your car or motorcycle.

3 A _____ is a place where you buy clothes and many other things.

4 A _____ is a place where you can wait for a bus.

5 A _____ is a place where you can buy a newspaper or a magazine.

8 Fill in the blanks with the correct tag questions.

RICCARDO: That department store is very big, ___isn't it___? And I've never seen so
(1)

many teen magazines!

SHELLEY: Oh...you stopped at the newsstand in front of the gas station,

_____?
(2)

RICCARDO: Yes, I did. You were in the drugstore, _____?
(3)

SHELLEY: Yes, I was. You got the cake, _____?
(4)

RICCARDO: Yes, I did. I got some balloons, too. That wasn't a bad idea,

_____?
(5)

SHELLEY: No, it wasn't! But we should hurry! The party is going to start in half an

hour, _____?
(6)

RICCARDO: Yes. But our bus stops at that bus stop, _____? Don't
(7)

worry, we won't be late.

9 Read the conversation in exercise 8 again. Fill in the blanks to write true sentences. Use the verbs and verb forms in parentheses and *not* (if necessary).

1 Riccardo _____went_____ to the newsstand. (*go / simple past*)

2 Shelley _____ at the newsstand with Riccardo. (*stop / simple past*)

3 Riccardo _____ a cake at the bakery. (*buy / simple past*)

4 The party _____ in three hours. (*start / future: going to*)

5 Shelley and Riccardo _____ to the bus stop. (*run / present progressive*)

10 Read the e-mail. Answer the questions in your notebook.

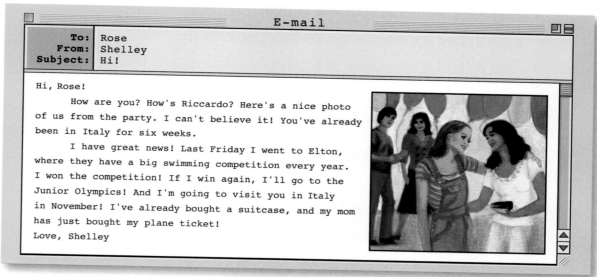

```
                              E-mail
     To:  Rose
   From:  Shelley
Subject:  Hi!

Hi, Rose!
     How are you? How's Riccardo? Here's a nice photo
of us from the party. I can't believe it! You've already
been in Italy for six weeks.
     I have great news! Last Friday I went to Elton,
where they have a big swimming competition every year.
I won the competition! If I win again, I'll go to the
Junior Olympics! And I'm going to visit you in Italy
in November! I've already bought a suitcase, and my mom
has just bought my plane ticket!
Love, Shelley
```

Example How long has Rose been in Italy?

She's been in Italy for six weeks.

1 Where are Shelley and Rose in the photo?
2 When did Shelley go to Elton?
3 What will happen if Shelley wins again?
4 What has Shelley already bought?
5 What has Shelley's mother just done?

Put it together!

11 Play a game. Work in pairs. Look through your book. Discuss your opinions about the most interesting story, the best character in the book, and the most difficult or easiest grammar point. Use tag questions.

Example STUDENT A: The story about the lost cat was the most interesting story, wasn't it?

STUDENT B: Yes, it was.

Rewind

① Match the sentences.

1 A chef is a person
2 A triangle is a shape
3 A mail carrier is a person
4 Mechanics are people
5 A stereo is a machine
6 A pilot is a person

A that has three sides.
B who can fly planes.
C that plays music.
D who cooks food.
E who fix cars.
F who delivers letters.

② Combine the sentences with *who* or *that*.

1 An ID card is a document. It shows information about you.

  An ID card is a document that shows information about you.

2 I have a brother. He is a musician.

  I have a brother who is a musician.

3 Danny bought a car. It was very old.

  _____

4 I'm going to meet a friend. She has just finished her exams.

  _____

5 Her father is a journalist. He works for the TV news.

  _____

6 Computers are machines. They can do many things.

  _____

③ Unscramble the letters and number the objects in the picture.

1 HOTSHRUBOT

2 TEAPOTSHOT

3 POSA

4 SHOPAMO

5 BURIHARSH

6 MOCB

1 ___toothbrush___
2 _____
3 _____
4 _____
5 _____
6 _____

4 Fill in the blanks with *who*, *where*, or *that*.

1 Let's go to the restaurant _____where_____ they make great pizza!

2 What do you call the place _____ you can see lots of animals?

3 A dentist is a person _____ fixes teeth.

4 That is the school _____ I learned to speak English.

5 Do you know a department store _____ I can buy a cheap TV?

6 What do you call the little machine _____ does math problems?

5 Fill in the blanks with the correct form of the verb in parentheses. Use the simple present, present progressive, present perfect, simple past, or future with *be* + *going to*.

JUNE: Hi, Ted. What _____are you doing_____ ?
(**1** *you / do*)

TED: I _____ for a cheap vacation.
(**2** *look*)

JUNE: Ooh, I _____ vacations!
(**3** *love*)

_____ to Florida?
(**4** *you / ever / be*)

TED: Yes, I _____ there last year.
(**5** *go*)

JUNE: I _____ to the United States.
(**6** *never / be*)

TED: It's great, but this summer I

_____ a new place.
(**7** *try*)

6 🎧 Listen to the song and fill in the blanks. Is the singer telling the truth?

I know a cool place where (**1**) ___banana___ trees grow

And the sun always shines. So come on, let's go!

We'll talk and we'll play with some (**2**) _____

I know.

You like cool places, don't you?

I have a (**3**) _____ that's a hundred meters tall.

There's a zoo in the yard, and there's gold

on the walls.

The living room's as big as a shopping mall.

You don't believe me, do you?

Transfer to Zoology

What kind of a cat is that?

1 **Read the descriptions of these cats in the magazine.**

Cornish Rex

This is a Cornish Rex cat. They are small and very thin. Their fur is short. They have big ears and long, thin legs. These cats can be many colors. Cornish Rex cats are very active. They love to play games.

Manx

The Manx cat is a cat with no tail. These cats came from the Isle of Man, near the coast of Britain. Manx cats have large round heads and bodies. Their back legs are longer than their front legs. They can jump very high. They also love to play.

Persian

Persian cats are very popular cats. People love their beautiful long fur. Persian cats have short legs. Because of this, they can't jump very high. These cats love their owners very much.

Now write CR (*Cornish Rex*), M (*Manx*), or P (*Persian*) next to each characteristic.

Long fur —	Most popular —	Big ears —
Very thin —	Short fur —	No tail —
Short legs —	Playful —, —	

2 **You are a writer for *Dogs!* magazine. Choose one of these dogs. Write a description in your notebook.**

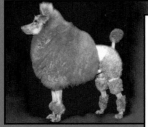

Project

What's your favorite pet? Find a picture. Write a description. Collect your class's descriptions in a class *Pets!* magazine.

Transfer to Geography

Volcanoes

1 Read Alex Pedrillo's report about volcanoes.

On my trip to Japan, I visited Mount Fuji. Mount Fuji is 3,776 meters high. It is a volcano. It isn't an active volcano. It's dormant. *Dormant* means that it is "sleeping." The last eruption of Mount Fuji was in 1707.

A volcano is a mountain made of lava. Lava is liquid rock that comes up from under the earth. When a volcano erupts (or explodes), hot, red lava comes out of the volcano. There is also a cloud of gas and ash. After an eruption, the lava cools and becomes hard rock. This rock forms the cone of the volcano.

There are more than 700 volcanoes around the world. Many of them are in the "Ring of Fire" around the Pacific Ocean. But there are volcanoes in Europe, too. There are also "new" volcanoes, in countries like Mexico and Iceland, that erupted in the 1900s.

2 In your notebook, answer the questions.

1 Is Mount Fuji an active volcano or a dormant volcano?

2 When was the last eruption of Mount Fuji?

3 About how many volcanoes are there in the world?

3 Label these items on the diagram of the volcano.

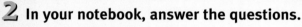

lava   ash cloud   cone

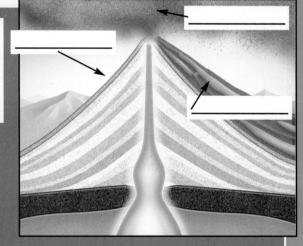

Project

Where are the volcanoes? Do some research. Then match the letters on the map with the volcano names.

VOLCANOES
_ **Paricutín**
_ **Hekla**
_ **Mount Etna**
_ **Mauna Loa**

● = volcano

Transfer to Drama

The Mystery in the Closet

Work in groups of five. Read the play. Each person should read a different part. Practice it several times. The narrator can make the sound effects.

Cast: Martha Jennings   Harry Jennings
Pamela Jennings   Roy Jennings

NARRATOR: It's 10 o'clock on a Saturday night. Martha Jennings, her husband Harry, and their children, Pamela and Roy, have just returned from the movies.

[*Sound: Door opening and closing*]

ROY: It's dark in here. Pam, turn on the light, please.

[*Sound: click of light switch*]

HARRY: Hey, guys, look. The refrigerator is open. Who did that?

PAM: I don't know, but he or she has eaten a piece of chocolate cake!

MARTHA: What a mess! Listen! I hear a noise. Who's there?

[*Sound: a very quiet sound, like a person moving*]

HARRY: I'll look.

PAM: Be careful.

[*Sound: slow footsteps*]

PAM: Look at the pieces of cake on the stairs. Maybe he's gone upstairs. Or she. Or it! Let's check.

[*Sound of footsteps going upstairs*]

ROY: Oh, no! Look at my room! My books and clothes are all on the floor.

PAM: Shhh. Listen! Do you hear that noise in the closet?

[*Sound: something moving and making strange but quiet sounds in the closet*]

ROY: Yes! What is it? Have you ever heard a sound like that?

HARRY: Look out! I'm going to open the door.

MARTHA: Oh, no!

Project

What or who is in the closet? Work with your group. Finish the story. Then present your play to the class. (If possible, record it on an audiocassette with the sound effects.)

Transfer to Language

How do you say *Good morning* in ...?

1 Here are some common world languages. The numbers represent the number of people who speak these languages as their first language. Complete the chart. Put the languages in order from the one with the most speakers to the one with the least.

Chinese (Mandarin) = 885 million

English = 322 million

French = 72 million

German = 98 million

Italian = 37 million

Japanese = 125 million

Polish = 44 million

Portuguese = 170 million

Spanish = 332 million

Swedish = 9 million

	Language	Number of speakers
1	Chinese	885 million
2		
3		
4		
5		
6		
7		
8		
9		
10		

2 Look at the expression *Good morning* in 8 different languages. Can you guess the languages? Fill in the blanks.

1	Chinese (Mandarin)	5	
2		6	
3		7	
4		8	

Project

Organize a panel discussion. Talk about the questions below with a group of your classmates. Then present your discussion to the class.

1 What's your first language?

2 What other languages do you speak?

3 What language(s) would you like to learn?

4 What languages might be most useful to you in the future? Why?

5 What languages do people in your community speak?

1 早安
zaov an-

2 Dzień dobry

3 Bonjour

4 Guten Morgen

5 Bom dia

6 God morgon

7 おはよう ございます
Ohayō gozaimasu

8 Buon giorno

Learning English My Way

Units 1–4
Learn English from a newspaper or magazine.

Things to do...

1 Get an English newspaper or magazine. Choose a short article or an advertisement.

2 Read the article or advertisement. What is it about?

3 Write a paragraph about it in English.

Units 5–8
Use English to plan a trip!

Things to do...

1 Visit a travel Web site. Get some information about a country you would like to visit. Try to get the information in English.

2 In English, write notes on things to do in that country.

3 Make a plan for a trip.

Units 9–12
Perform in English!

Things to do...

1 With some friends, choose a short and easy story or play from your own language. Think about the story in English.

2 Write a dialog in English.

3 Act the dialog with your friends. You can use props—for example, telephones, costumes, etc.

Week 1	I'll review my planner from last year and choose the most helpful plans. I will practice them.
Week 2	I'll choose 10 new English words. I'll ask my friends about their meanings. Then we'll check them in a dictionary.
Week 3	I'll review English grammar. I'll review irregular simple past forms and past participle forms.

Examples	come	came	come
	write	wrote	written
	put	put	put

Units 13–16
Continue learning English during the summer.

Things to do...

Last summer you made a planner for learning English over the summer. This summer make a new planner and use it.

Grammar at a Glance

Past habits: *used to* / *didn't use to* + verb

	AFFIRMATIVE	NEGATIVE
singular	I You **used to** walk to work. He/She/It	I You **didn't use to** drive to work. He/She/It
plural	We You **used to** walk to work. They	We You **didn't use to** drive to work. They

Note: There is no *-d* on the word *use* in the negative form *didn't use to*.

Agreeing and disagreeing: *too* and *not... either*

AGREE	DISAGREE
A: I like chocolate. B: I do, **too**!	A: I like chocolate. B: I **don't**!
A: I don't like coffee. B: I don't, **either**!	A: I don't like coffee. B: I **do**!

A few, a little, a lot of

COUNTABLE	UNCOUNTABLE
I have **a few** books. He has **a lot of** books.	Let's use **a little** salt. Don't use **a lot of** salt!

Note: Use *a lot of* with both countable and uncountable nouns.

Reflexive pronouns

	SUBJECT PRONOUN	REFLEXIVE PRONOUN
singular	I you he she it	myself yourself himself herself itself
plural	we you they	ourselves yourselves themselves

First conditional: *if*

IF-CLAUSE (SIMPLE PRESENT)	MAIN CLAUSE (*WILL* + VERB)
If he asks me,	I'll **help** him.
If he plays well,	he **will win** the game.
If we don't leave now,	we'll **be** late.

First conditional: information questions

QUESTION WORD + MAIN CLAUSE	IF-CLAUSE
What will you do	if I don't help you?
When will Bob arrive	if he leaves at 7 o'clock?
Who will meet us	if we're late?

Grammar at a Glance

Modal verbs

ADVICE: *SHOULD (NOT)* + VERB

The party is formal. You **should wear** a jacket and tie.
The class is at 8 o'clock. We **should leave** the house at 7.
Shhh! You **shouldn't talk** during the movie.

OBLIGATION: *MUST (NOT)* + VERB

He's going to Europe. He **must take** a passport.
You **must not give** that medicine to a child. It's for adults.

POSSIBILITY: *MIGHT (NOT)* + VERB

Alex **might** go to Egypt.
He **might not win** the contest.

Note: *should + not = shouldn't*
must + not = mustn't
might + not = mightn't (BUT people don't often use
this form in American English.)

Obligation: *have to / (not) have to*

I / You / We / They	have to don't have to	work today.
He / She / It	has to doesn't have to	work tomorrow.

Gerunds: verb + *-ing* used as a noun

Swimming is fun.
I like **swimming**.

Note: The gerund (verb + *-ing*) is different from the
present progressive, *be* + verb + *-ing*.
Compare these sentences:
He is **reading**. (present progressive)
Reading is interesting. (gerund)

How + adjective / adverb: questions

How tall are the Pyramids
How far is Paris from Rome?

Units 9–12

Present perfect: statements

I You We They	have (not)	helped them.
He She It	has (not)	helped them.

Short forms:
I have = I've   *have not = haven't*
he has = he's   *has not = hasn't*
Note: *He's* can mean *He has* or *He is*
(look for the past participle to
identify the present perfect).

Present perfect: *yes/no* questions

YES/NO QUESTIONS			SHORT ANSWERS					
Have	I you we they	worked?	Yes,	I you we they	have.	No,	I you we they	haven't.
Has	he she it	worked?	Yes,	he she it	has.	No,	he she it	hasn't.

Present perfect: information questions

QUESTION WORD	*HAVE/HAS*	SUBJECT	PARTICIPLE
What	have	I / you / we / they	done?
What	has	he / she / it	done?

Grammar at a Glance

Words used with the present perfect

EVER / NEVER

Have you **ever** read that book?
I've **never** seen that movie.
The word *ever* is used in questions. The word *never* is negative.

FOR / SINCE

I've studied English **for** four years.
We've been here **since** March.
Use *for* with a period of time. Use *since* with a specific time.

JUST / ALREADY / YET

He has **just** written a letter.
She has **already** done the homework.
You haven't been there **yet**.

just = a short time ago
already = previously, before now
not...yet = <u>not</u> up to this time

Tag questions: *be*

AFFIRMATIVE	NEGATIVE
I'm on time,	**aren't** I?*
He's tall,	**isn't** he?
They're friends,	**aren't** they?
I was at home,	**wasn't** I?
You were scared,	**weren't** you?
We were there,	**weren't** we?

NEGATIVE	AFFIRMATIVE
I'm **not** a student,	**am** I?
He **isn't** American,	**is** he?
We **aren't** swimmers,	**are** we?
You **weren't** angry,	**were** you?
She **wasn't** on the team,	**was** she?

*Do not use *am not* in tag questions.

Tag questions: other verbs

AFFIRMATIVE	NEGATIVE
You like hamburgers,	**don't** you?
He lives in Brazil,	**doesn't** he?
She ate the last cookie,	**didn't** she?
We had a good time,	**didn't** we?

NEGATIVE	AFFIRMATIVE
I **don't** know you,	**do** I?
She **doesn't** like pizza,	**does** she?
You **didn't** write to him,	**did** you?
They **didn't** take pictures,	**did** they?

Relative clauses

WHO

A vet is a doctor. **He/She** takes care of animals.
  A vet is a doctor **who** takes care of animals.

THAT

A subway is a train. **It** travels under the ground.
  A subway is a train **that** travels under the ground.

WHERE

We went to the bakery. They make bread **at the bakery**.
  We went to the bakery **where** they make bread.

1 **Unscramble the letters in parentheses. Match 1–5 with A–E.**

1 fur
   (u/f/r)

2 _____
   (a/b/c/k)

3 _____
   (w/a/p/s)

4 _____
   (l/a/i/t)

5 _____
   (t/a/p/h/c)

A A dog moves this when it's happy.

B A cat uses these to walk.

C It's a different color.

D This is the hair on animals.

E You sit on this part of a horse.

2 **What did Cathy do this morning? What didn't she do? Look at the ✓s (things she did) and Xs (things she didn't do). Write sentences with the words in parentheses. (✓ = did and X = didn't)**

1 X (wake up at 6)   She didn't wake up at 6 o'clock.

2 ✓ (finish her homework)   She finished her homework.

3 X (take a shower)   _____

4 X (have breakfast)   _____

5 ✓ (ride her bicycle)   _____

6 X (clean her room)   _____

3 **Complete the dialog. Use the words in parentheses and the simple past.**

TERRY: Did you and Ed go to the movies last weekend?
        (1 you and Ed / go / to the movies last weekend)

LAURIE: No, _____ .
        (2 we / not)

        _____ to the museum.
        (3 we / go)

TERRY: Oh. _____ there?
        (4 what / you / see)

LAURIE: _____ the dinosaur exhibit.
        (5 we / see)

TERRY: _____ a souvenir?
        (6 you / buy)

LAURIE: Yes, I did. Look! Isn't it great?

TERRY: A dinosaur! How cute!

Plus Practice

1 What were these people doing at 8 P.M. yesterday? Look at the chart and complete the sentences.

PERSON	ACTIVITY
Sue	write an e-mail
Patrick	eat dinner
Dad	wash the dishes
Peter and Jack	listen to music
We	play tennis
Grandpa	fix the armchair

1 Sue _____ was writing an e-mail _____ .

2 Patrick _____ .

3 Dad _____ .

4 Peter and Jack _____ .

5 We _____ .

6 Grandpa _____ .

2 Fill in the blanks with the words below.

> relieved   thrilled   worried   embarrassed   disappointed

1 She was _____ thrilled _____ because her friends gave her a surprise party.

2 He was _____ when he did very well on the test.

3 We were _____ because our dream trip was too expensive.

4 I fell in the cafeteria, and everyone saw me. I was so _____ !

5 They were _____ because their child was in the hospital.

3 Sam and Cathy are planning a trip. How are they going to make enough money? Write the sentences with the words in parentheses and *be + going to*.

1 Cathy is going to work at a store. _____
       (Cathy / work at a store)

2 _____
       (Cathy and Sam / clean their aunt's garage)

3 _____
       (Cathy / not buy candy for three months)

4 _____
       (Sam and Cathy / not go to the movies for two months)

5 _____
       (Sam / wash his neighbor's dog)

6 _____
       (Cathy / not buy new shoes)

1 **What did the three friends think of the movie? Fill in the blanks with *afraid,*** **_ridiculous, pretty,_ or *scary*.**

ANN: Did you like the movie?

BETTY: I liked it, but it was ___scary___ . All those

cockroaches...

MARK: I think they were cool. Weren't they

_____? I'd like to have a pet

cockroach.

ANN: Don't be _____ ! I closed my

eyes because I was so _____ ....

Hey, Mark, look! A cockroach on your back!

MARK: Eek! Help!

2 **What used to be true about Mark, Ann, and Betty in the past? Complete the** **sentences.**

1 Mark _used to be afraid of scary movies_ . Now he watches scary movies.

2 Betty and Mark _____ . Now they are good friends.

3 Betty _____ . Now she isn't heavy.

4 Ann _____ . Now she eats hamburgers.

5 Ann and Mark _____ . Now they aren't afraid of big dogs.

6 Ann _____ . Now she is tall.

3 **Mark, Betty, and Ann have a lot in common. Fill in the blanks with *too* or *either*.**

1 Ann goes to school in the morning. Betty and Mark do, ___too___ .

2 Betty lives in High Mountain. Mark does, _____ .

3 Mark doesn't like math. Betty doesn't, _____ .

4 Ann and Mark have a bicycle. Betty does, _____ .

5 Ann doesn't drive. Mark and Betty don't, _____ .

6 Betty likes video games. Mark and Ann do, _____ .

Plus Practice

1 **Circle the "odd" word in each group.**

1 worried	thrilled	(bed)	disappointed
2 lake	pool	river	mountain
3 shirt	dress	salad dressing	jeans
4 mustard	pepper	soy sauce	orange juice
5 kitten	nurse	mail carrier	shopkeeper

2 **The Stuarts bought some food at the supermarket. Write _T_ (_True_) or _F_ (_False_), and correct the false sentences.**

1 They bought a little soy sauce.   (**F**)

They bought a lot of soy sauce.

2 They bought a little salt.   ( )

_____

3 They bought a little salad dressing.   ( )

_____

4 They bought a lot of pepper.   ( )

_____

5 They bought a few jars of mustard.   ( )

_____

6 They bought an apple.   ( )

_____

3 **What happened to the Stuarts at 3 P.M. yesterday? Write sentences with the simple past of the verbs in parentheses and _herself, himself, itself,_ or _themselves._**

1 Melanie jumped and fell.   She hurt herself.
                                          (_hurt_)

2 Dad cooked hot food. _____
                                          (_burn_)

3 Mom opened a can of soda. _____
                                          (_cut_)

4 The children swam in the lake. _____
                                          (_enjoy_)

5 The cat walked on the food. _____
                                          (_not / behave_)

6 Ben got dirty. _____
                                          (_wash_)

1 Fill in the blanks with the words in the box. Then put the sentences in order.

> deliver   envelopes   mail carrier   receive   addresses   stamps

Justin wants to invite all his friends to his birthday party. This is his plan:

___ **A** I'll send the cards. The _____ will _____ the invitations to

my friends in about two days.

_1_ **B** First, I need to buy the cards, some _____envelopes_____ , and

_____ .

___ **C** When they _____ the invitations, they will be surprised.

___ **D** Next, I'll write the cards, and after that, I'll write my friends' names and

_____ on the envelopes.

2 Clara and Penny are talking about Justin's party. Fill in the blanks with the correct form of the verbs in parentheses.

CLARA: If I ___receive___ an invitation, I'___ll go___ .
                  (**1** *receive*)   (**2** *go*)

PENNY: Yes! If we _____ , we
                     (**3** *not / go*)

_____ a great party!
     (**4** *miss*)

CLARA: But if we _____ , we
                  (**5** *go*)

_____ some new clothes. And a
     (**6** *need*)

gift for Justin.

PENNY: Who _____ us if it
            (**7** *drive*)

_____ ?
     (**8** *rain*)

CLARA: My brother. And if he _____ us,
                        (**9** *not / take*)

I _____ my mom.
   (**10** *ask*)

3 Match 1–4 with A–D.

  1 Justin will be disappointed
  2 Justin will be thrilled
  3 Penny and Clara will be happy
  4 Justin's mother will be worried

  A if many people come to his party.
  B if they find a beautiful gift for Justin.
  C if the party is very noisy.
  D if Clara doesn't come.

Plus Practice

1 Read Adrian's checklist. Check (✓) the things on the list that you can see in Adrian's room.

DON'T FORGET!!
1 jacket ✓
1 suit
2 belts
1 tie
2 T-shirts
3 shirts
2 socks

2 Adrian is going to stay at a friend's apartment in Los Angeles. What *should* or *shouldn't* Adrian do? Circle the correct word in parentheses.

1 He ((should)/shouldn't) give a gift to his friend.

2 He (should / shouldn't) arrive late.

3 He (should / shouldn't) help his friend with the dishes.

4 He (should / shouldn't) use the phone too much.

5 He (should / shouldn't) clean his room.

6 He (should / shouldn't) learn English.

3 What are the rules of good driving? Write sentences with *must* or *mustn't* and the words in parentheses.

1 (drive carefully)   Drivers must drive carefully.

2 (stop at the red light)   _____

3 (read a book while driving) _____

4 (watch the road)   _____

5 (know all the signs)   _____

1 What's in the "alphabet" soup? Make vegetable words from the word parts in the soup. Then write the words in the correct blanks below.

1 _____onion_____ It's not sad, but it can make you cry.

2 _____ It looks like a small tree.

3 _____ Some of them are dangerous.

4 _____ It's orange, but it's not an orange.

5 _____ It's half a plant and half an egg.

[soup can labels: BROCC ROT, EGG ROOMS, MUSH ION, ON OLI, CAR PLANT]

2 Complete the answers using *might*.

1 Where are you going this weekend?

I'm not sure. I _____might go_____ to the beach.

2 Who is the man next to Chris?

I'm not sure. He _____ his friend.

3 Where do they take the bus?

I'm not sure. They _____ across from the library.

4 When will Lisa prepare her presentation?

I'm not sure. She. _____ today.

3 Complete with the correct form of *have to* and the words in parentheses.

1 My pet is sick. I _____have to take him to the vet_____ .
(take him to the vet)

2 Her computer isn't working. She _____ .
(fix it)

3 Tomorrow is Sunday. They _____ .
(not / wake up early)

4 My birthday party is tomorrow night. My mom _____ .
(bake a cake)

5 You are not traveling to another country. You _____ .
(not / use your passport)

Plus Practice

(1) Read the hotel ad. Fill in the blanks under the pictures with the words from the box.

> fishing   hiking   horseback riding   rock climbing

Come to Great Time Hotels and enjoy nature!

1 _____

2 _____

3 _____

4 _____

(2) Complete the sentences with the gerunds of the verbs in parentheses.

1 (*ride bicycles*)   <u>Riding bicycles</u> is easy.

2 (*talk*)   Is _____ to strangers dangerous?

3 (*play drums*)   _____ can be difficult.

4 (*feed hippopotamuses*)   Are you afraid of _____ ?

5 (*camp*)   _____ in the forest is fun.

(3) Fill in the blanks with the correct adjective from the box.

> big   far   long   old   tall

1 How __tall__ are you?   — I'm 1.80 meters tall.

2 How _____ is Tokyo?   — It's very big.

3 How _____ do you live from Dallas?   — 20 kilometers.

4 How _____ was the tennis game?   — About an hour.

5 How _____ is your brother?   — Older than you.

6 How _____ is that tree?   — Over 15 meters.

Plus Practice

1 **Do you know your school subjects? Match 1–5 with A–E.**

   1 art

   2 biology

   3 physical education

   4 chemistry

   5 geography

   A Asia, Europe, Africa

   B plants and animals

   C Picasso, Rodin, Goya

   D basketball, volleyball, baseball

   E H_2O = water

2 **The information about Bill, Phil, and Will is false. Make true statements by writing the opposite of each sentence. Then label each picture with the right name.**

   1 Bill has played basketball all day.

      <u>No, Bill hasn't played basketball all day.</u>

   2 Phil and Will have played tennis today.

   3 Will hasn't listened to rock music today.

   4 Phil hasn't gone to art class today.

A   **B**   **C**

3 **Fill in the blanks with the present perfect form of the verbs in parentheses.**

Bill   <u>has driven</u>   to the sports center many times. He _____
       (1 drive**)**   **(2** play**)**

tennis all his life. Will _____ to rock music all his life. But he
                      (3 listen**)**

_____ classical music CDs before. Phil _____
   (4 not buy**)**   **(5** love**)**

art all his life. He _____ many pictures, and _____
                  (6 paint**)**   **(7** visit**)**

many art museums.

Plus Practice

1 Look at the map and complete the sentences with *north, south, east,* or *west.*

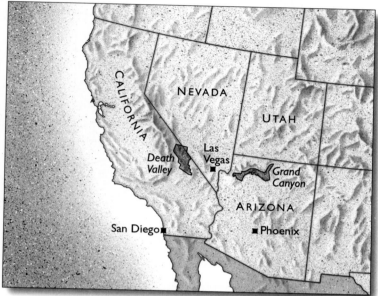

1 Las Vegas is ___east___ of Death Valley.

2 Las Vegas is _____ of the Grand Canyon.

3 Phoenix is _____ of the Grand Canyon.

4 Death Valley is _____ of San Diego.

2 Match questions 1–5 with answers A–E.
1 Has Nan gone to the baseball game?
2 Have you read this novel, Jean?
3 Has Rick driven the new car?
4 Have Karen and Tom watched a comedy show?
5 Have you and Mary done the project?

A No, we haven't.
B Yes, he has.
C No, she hasn't.
D Yes, I have.
E No, they haven't.

3 Write the questions.

1 <u>Have you been to Belgium?</u> — No, we've never been to Belgium.

2 _____ — Yes, she's finished the test.

3 _____ — Yes, he's bought the car.

4 _____ — No, I've never said that.

5 _____ — Yes, they've told her.

4 Write about yourself. Use long answers.

1 Have you ever played golf? — <u>Yes, I have played golf.</u> *or*
   <u>No, I have never played golf.</u>

2 Have you ever taken karate lessons? — _____

3 Have you ever seen an ostrich? — _____

4 Have you ever been to Caracas? — _____

5 Have you ever eaten *tempura*? — _____

Plus Practice

1 **How many different shapes can you count?**

1 There are _____thirty-two_____ triangles.

2 There are _____ rectangles.

3 There are _____ diamonds.

4 There are _____ stars.

5 There are _____ hearts.

6 There are _____ squares.

7 There are _____ circles.

2 ***Since*** **or** ***for*?** **Circle the correct alternative.**

1 I haven't played the piano (_since_ / _for_) last year.

2 Brenda hasn't bought new CDs (_since_ / _for_) September.

3 You've studied biology (_since_ / _for_) six years.

4 Charlie and I have walked (_since_ / _for_) two hours.

5 Danny hasn't seen her (_since_ / _for_) eight o'clock.

6 The cats have eaten this cat food (_since_ / _for_) four years.

3 **Complete the questions with** ***What, Who,*** **or** ***Where.***

1 _____What_____ have you cooked?   —   Fish and fries.

2 _____ have Lesley and Gary worked?   —   At the bookstore.

3 _____ has Yuri met at the airport?   —   A friend.

4 _____ has Mary written?   —   A letter to her mom.

5 _____ have I put my wallet?   —   I don't know!

6 _____ has he gone to lunch with?   —   His brother.

4 **Write questions with** ***How long.***

1 How long has she been an artist?   —   She has been an artist for ten years.

2 _____   —   He has been on the team since January.

3 _____   —   They have lived here for three months.

4 _____   —   You have been at work for two hours.

99

Plus Practice

1 Look at the chart. Write what Jack's mother has already done and what she hasn't done yet.

1 <u>She has already vacuumed the living room.</u>

2 <u>She hasn't cleaned the windows yet.</u>

3 _____

4 _____

5 _____

6 _____

vacuum the living room	✓
clean the windows	X
wash the dishes	✓
water the plants	X
make the beds	X
clean the bathroom	✓

2 It's 7 P.M. and Jack is relaxing. Continue the story. Put the words in order to write the sentences.

1 <u>Jack has just turned on the TV.</u>
      (the TV / turned on / has / Jack / . / just)

2 _____
      (started / . / yet / The movie / hasn't)

3 _____
      (. / just / arrived / Sam and Julia / have)

4 _____
      (this movie / They / yet / . / haven't / watched)

5 _____
      (started / just / The movie / has / .)

6 _____
      (But / has / . / fallen asleep / Jack / just)

3 Read the sentences in exercises 1 and 2.
Match the questions to the answers.

1 Has Sam ever seen this movie?   **A** We don't know.
2 Who has cleaned the house?   **B** Sam.
3 Who has come with Julia?   **C** Jack's mother.
4 Has Jack seen this movie already?   **D** No, he hasn't.

Plus Practice

1 Match 1–5 with A–E.

1 I've just tried the chicken. It ___tastes___ wonderful!

2 Doesn't Peter _____ bored in that picture?

3 Who's playing the saxophone? It _____ awful!

4 How cold is the water? Can you _____ it?

5 Whose socks are these? They _____ bad!

A smell

B feel

C look

D tastes

E sounds

2 Find the mistakes. Write the corrections.

1 I am a good student, ~~am not~~ I?   ___aren't___

2 Sally isn't going to Italy, is Sally?   _____

3 I am not the winner, I'am?   _____

4 Jim and Mike are very angry, isn't it?   _____

5 Tessie and I are not going sailing, aren't we? _____

6 The fire station is not near, isn't it?   _____

3 Complete the conversation with tag questions.

POLICEMAN: Your name is Nick,

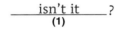
(1) ___isn't it___?

NICK: Yes, it is.

POLICEMAN: And you were at the bank at

3 P.M., _____ ?
(2)

NICK: No, I wasn't.

POLICEMAN: You were in the car outside the

bank, _____ ?
(3)

NICK: No, I wasn't. I was watching the baseball game on TV!

POLICEMAN: That's not true, _____ , Nick? You weren't watching the
(4)

baseball game at 3 P.M., _____ ? You and your partner
(5)

were stealing the money from the bank!

Plus Practice

1 **Look at the picture. Fill in the blanks with the names of the objects.**

1 _____towel_____

2 _____

3 _____

4 _____

5 _____

2 **Fill in the blanks with the correct tag questions.**

DONNA: You saw me at the pool, _____didn't you_____?
(1)

KIM: Yes, I did. Why?

DONNA: You saw my goggles there, _____?
(2)

KIM: Yes, I did.

DONNA: I dried myself with my towel, _____?
(3)

KIM: Yes, you did.

DONNA: And we were both wearing bathing caps, _____?
(4)

KIM: Yes, we were.

DONNA: And my bathrobe was on a chair, _____?
(5)

KIM: Yes, it was.

DONNA: Oh, no! I left all those things at the pool!

3 **Match 1–5 with A–E.**

1 You don't have to go,   **A** is it?

2 John doesn't run every day,   **B** do they?

3 Diving isn't easy,   **C** do you?

4 Cats don't like water,   **D** don't they?

5 They wear funny clothes,   **E** does he?

Plus Practice

1 What do these people need to do the activities? Use the objects below to complete the sentences.

    1 Melanie is going to take a shower. <u>She'll need some soap.</u>

    2 I am going to brush my hair. ──────────────

    3 You are going to wash your hair. ──────────────

    4 We are going to comb our hair. ──────────────

    5 Artie, Lori, and Rob are going to brush their teeth. ──────────────

2 Match 1–4 with A–D. Then rewrite the sentences using *who* or *that*.

    1 A banana is a fruit   **A** helps animals.
    2 A camera is a thing   **B** interviews people.
    3 A reporter is a person   **C** takes pictures.
    4 A vet is a person   **D** is long and yellow.

    1 <u>A banana is a fruit that is long and yellow.</u>

    2 ──────────────

    3 ──────────────

    4 ──────────────

3 Write definitions for the words below using *who* or *that*.

    1 A goat is   <u>an animal that eats many different foods.</u>

    2 A baker is ──────────────.

    3 A bookstore is ──────────────.

    4 A principal is ──────────────.

    5 A playground is ──────────────.

    6 A pencil is ──────────────.

Plus Practice

1 **Where did the people go? Unscramble the letters of their names and find out.**

> gas station   department store   drugstore   newsstand   bus stop

1 TERESA PORTTMEND _____department store_____

2 BOSS TUP _____

3 TONI STAGAS _____

4 GUS DORRET _____

5 STAN SWEND _____

2 **Look at the pictures and labels. Then complete sentences 1-5 using *is a place where*.**

get money

eat dinner

get on a plane

listen to music

buy bread

1 A concert hall _____is a place where you can listen to music._____

2 A bakery _____ .

3 A restaurant _____ .

4 A bank _____ .

5 An airport _____ .

3 **Fill in the blanks with *who*, *where*, or *that*.**

1 A bed is a place __where__ you can sleep.

2 The vet helped the pig _____ was sick.

3 My cousins are the students _____ won the prize.

4 An actor is a person _____ works in movies.

5 Africa is the place _____ many lions live.

Wordmaster

This list shows the new key words and phrases in this book and where they are introduced. Use the list to practice them. Draw pictures or write sentences with the words. Or write a definition.

KEY

Numbers in bold = Unit numbers

Other numbers = exercise numbers

T = Tip

Aa
a little **4**-5 _____
a lot of **4**-5 _____
about **1**-1 _____
afraid **3**-1 _____
again **2**-6 _____
agree **6**-10 _____
already **12**-1 ___He has already arrived.___
another **14**-1 _____
anymore **13**-4 _____
architecture **8**-1 _____
avenue **1**-8 _____

Bb
back **1**-7 _____
backyard **13**-1 _____
bakery **16**-1 _____
balloon **11**-1 _____
band **13**-8 _____
bathing cap **14**-5 _____
bathing suit **14**-5 _____
bathrobe **14**-5 _____
behave **4**-1 _____
believe **2**-1 _____
belt **6**-6 _____
bring **6**-1 _____
broccoli **7**-6 _____
brush **15**-8 _____
bus stop **16**-6 _____

Cc
camel **8**-1 _____
camping **8**-6 _____
care **4**-1 _____
carrot **7**-6 _____
cat food **1**-6 _____
character **10**-1 _____
chemistry **9**-5 _____

chopstick **7**-1 _____
circle **11**-2 _____
classical **3**-4 _____
climb **8**-6 _____
collection **5**-7 _____
comb **15**-7 _____
committee **5**-1 _____
company **9**-9 _____
competition **5**T _____
conference **5**-1 _____
coral **8**-1 _____
costume **12**-3 _____
creepy **3**-1 _____
cut **4**-1 _____

Dd
deliver **5**-7 _____
department store **16**-7 _____
diamond **11**-2 _____
disappointed **2**-1 _____
discussion **5**-1 _____
doorbell **3**-6 _____
document **15**-1 _____
drugstore **16**-7 _____
dry **4**-1 _____
during **6**-1 _____

Ee
east **10**-8 _____
eggplant **7**-6 ___= a purple vegetable___
either **3**-1 _____
embarrassed **2**-6 _____
emergency **6**-10 _____
enjoy **1**-2 _____
entire **14**-1 _____
envelope **5**-7 _____
ever **10**-1 _____
excellent **7**-1 _____

Wordmaster

exhilarating **8**-1 _____

exotic **8**-1 _____

Ff

far **8**-1 _____

fascinating **8**-1 _____

fault **9**-1 _____

feel **13**-7 _____

few **4**-5 _____

flight **6**-7 _____

focus **7**-8 _____

follow **1**-1 _____

following **6**-1 _____

formal **6**-1 _____

fur **1**-7 _____

Gg

gas station **16**-7 _____

gasoline **16**-7 _____

geography **9**-5 _____

German **10**-5 _____

goggles **14**-5 _____

grammar **16**-1 _____

Grandma **1**-4 _____

Grandpa **1**-4 _____

group **7**-8 _____

grow **13**-1 _____

guideline **6**-1 _____

Hh

hairbrush **15**-7 _____

haircut **13**-8 _____

have to **7**-1 _____

heart **11**-1 _____

here **3**-1 _____

herself **4**-3 _____

hike **8**-6 _____

himself **4**-1 _____ Sammy hurt himself. _____

horseback riding **8**-6 _____

host **6**-1 _____

hurt **2**-6 _____

Ii

if **5**-1 _____

instruction **6**-1 _____

into **2**-10 _____

itself **4**-3 _____

Jj

jacket **6**-1 _____

jog **6**-4 _____

junior **16**-10 _____

just **9**-1 _____

Kk

keep **1**-5 _____

kilometer **8**-7 _____

kind of **6**-1 _____

kitten **4**-7 _____

knock **3**-6 _____

Korean **7**-8 _____

Ll

laugh **2**-1 _____

Mm

mail **5**-7 _____

member **5**-1 _____

might **7**-1 _____

mushroom **7**-6 _____

must **6**-1 _____

mustard **4**-5 _____

myself **4**-1 _____

Nn

national **10**-5 _____

near **8**-6 _____

nervous **12**-3 _____

newspaper **12**-3 _____

newsstand **16**-7 _____

north **10**-8 _____

novel **10**-1 _____

Oo

object **15**-9 _____

occasion **6**-1 _____

occupation **5**-9 _____

Wordmaster

onion **7**-6 _____
ourselves **4**-3 _____
owner **1**-1 _____

Pp
package **6**-7 _____
pass **3**-1 _____
passport **6**-7 _____
paste **15**-8 _____
patch **1**-7 _____
paw **1**-7 _____
peephole **3**-6 _____
pepper **4**-5 _____
performance **7**-8 _____
phone **11**-1 _____
photo album **15**-1 _____
physical education **9**-5 _____
play **10**-1 _____
plenty **8**-1 _____
polite **6**-1 _____
pool **4**-1 _____
popular **8**-1 _____
practice **11**-7 _____
prepare **7**-4 _____
presentation **5**-1 _____
pretty **3**-1 _____
problem **6**-1 _____
production **12**-1 _____
program **5**-3 _____
public **12**-3 _____
pueblo **8**-7 _____
purple **7**-6 _____
put away **12**-5 _____

Rr
raw **6**-1 _____
receive **5**-7 _____
recognize **5**-8 _____
rectangle **11**-2 _____
relieved **2**-6 = not worried _____
remember **2**-7 _____
represent **5**-1 _____
return address **5**-7 _____
review **12**-1 _____

ridiculous **3**-1 _____
ring **3**-6 _____
rule **6**-1 _____

Ss
salad dressing **4**-5 _____
salt **4**-5 _____
same **5**-8 _____
sashimi **6**-1 _____
scared **3**-1 _____
scuba dive **8**-1 _____
serve **6**-1 _____
set **12**-1 _____
shampoo **15**-7 _____
shape **11**-1 _____
should **6**-1 _____
since **11**-1 _____
slipper **6**-6 _____
smell **13**-1 _____
so **2**-6 _____
soap **15**-7 _____
song **13**-7 _____
soon **14**-1 _____
sound **13**-7 _____
south **10**-1 _____
soy sauce **4**-5 _____
square **11**-2 _____
stamp **5**-7 _____
star **11**-2 _____
state **8**-7 _____
still **14**-4 _____
stop **3**-6 _____
stranger **6**-7 _____
student representative **5**-1 _____
subject **9**-5 _____
suit **6**-6 _____
suitcase **15**-5 _____

Tt
take care of **4**-1 _____
taste **13**-7 _____
tempura **7**-5 _____
themselves **4**-3 _____
think **2**-6 _____

Wordmaster

thrilled **2**-6 _____

thrilling **8**-2 _____

tie **6**-6 _____

toothbrush **15**-7 _____

toothpaste **15**-7 _____

towel **14**-5 _____

traveler **6**-7 _____

triangle **11**-2 _____

turn on **12**-5 _____

turn off **12**-5 _____

Uu

underwater **8**-1 _____

unlock **4**-7 _____

upset **14**-1 _____

used to **3**-1 _____

Vv

vegetable **7**-6 _____

vocabulary **16**-1 _____

Ww

warm **6**-1 _____

wear **3**-4 _____

west **10**-8 ____California is west of Florida.____

wet **4**-1 _____

What a relief! **2**-6 _____

What's the matter? **12**-1 _____

word **6**-9 _____

World Cup **10**-5 _____

worried **2**-6 _____

Yy

yet **12**-1 _____

young **5**-9 _____

yourself **4**-1 _____

yourselves **4**-1 _____

Wordmaster

IRREGULAR VERBS IN THE PAST		
Base form	**Simple past**	**Past participle**
be	was/were	been
become	became	become
bring	brought	brought
buy	bought	bought
catch	caught	caught
choose	chose	chosen
come	came	come
cut	cut	cut
dig	dug	dug
do	did	done
drive	drove	driven
eat	ate	eaten
fall	fell	fallen
feel	felt	felt
find	found	found
forget	forgot	forgotten
get	got	gotten
give	gave	given
go	went	gone
grow	grew	grown
have	had	had
hit	hit	hit
hold	held	held
hurt	hurt	hurt
keep	kept	kept
know	knew	known
leave	left	left
make	made	made
meet	met	met
put	put	put
read	read	read
ride	rode	ridden
see	saw	seen
sell	sold	sold
send	sent	sent
show	showed	shown
sing	sang	sung
sit	sat	sat
sleep	slept	slept
speak	spoke	spoken
stand	stood	stood
steal	stole	stolen
swim	swam	swum
take	took	taken
teach	taught	taught
tell	told	told
think	thought	thought
wake	woke	woken
wear	wore	worn
win	won	won
write	wrote	written